MANDATE TO WITNESS

MANDATE

TO

WITNESS

STUDIES IN THE BOOK OF ACTS

Leander E. Keck

JUDSON PRESS

VALLEY FORGE •

International Standard Book Number 0-8170-0322-3
Library of Congress Catalog Card No. 64-15796

Seventh Printing, 1974

CONTENTS

For a faithful witness
THE REVEREND JOSEPH E. O'DONNELL, JR.
former classmate and pastor

FOREWORD

TODAY'S CHURCH HAS AN OVERSUPPLY OF ANALYSES AND OF exhortations — even excoriations. Most of it is warranted. Moreover, in the face of the various kinds of revolution and reactions to revolution which mark our era, many Christians have a growing sense of futility. This book intends to deal briefly with such concerns. It argues that, because important aspects of our situation were also present when the church was first launched, studying Acts can show that despair is not inevitable and that we may take heart from our ancient precedent. In short, this book is built on the conviction that our situation can be indeed an occasion for dismay and anxiety when we measure today's church against the memory of yesterday's Christendom. But when our situation is placed alongside that of the frontiersmen of the faith, ours is an occasion for forms of vitality which were impossible in Christendom.

The loss of Christendom must not cause Christians to take up the chant of Psalm 137:

> . . . *we sat down and wept,*
> *when we remembered Zion.*

Instead, they must hear the poet of Israel's exile sing the hymn of Isaiah 43:

"You are my witnesses," says the Lord,
"and my servant whom I have chosen,
that you may know and believe me
and understand that I am He." . . .

"Remember not the former things,
nor consider the things of old.
Behold, I am doing a new thing;
now it springs forth, do you not perceive it?"

The erosion of Christian culture as we have known it is not an invitation to weep, but a summons to go to work — not to salvage what we can, but to bear witness to him who has his own way of bringing to pass his will — even for our own times.

These studies (in an earlier form) were presented as lectures, in the summer of 1962, to the Adult Conference of the Tennessee Disciples of Christ at Bethany Hills, Tennessee, and to the American Baptist Ministers' Conference at Green Lake, Wisconsin. The discussions that these occasions provided helped to clarify many matters. Two colleagues read the manuscript and offered penetrating critiques, Professor James Sellers of Vanderbilt and Professor Gordon Kaufman, now at Harvard Divinity School. A word of appreciation must be recorded concerning the typists, Mrs. John McMahon and Mrs. James Gilliam, whose readiness to help meet deadlines is deeply appreciated.

LEANDER E. KECK

The Divinity School
Vanderbilt University
Nashville, Tennessee

HOW TO USE THIS BOOK

Directions come with the package, whether it is a cake mix, antique auto assembly kit or dry-pack car batteries. And now they come with books too! There is a difference, however. The manufacturer of a ready-to-assemble kit often says that, if the directions are followed, he will guarantee satisfaction or a refund. An author, unfortunately, cannot make such a promise. These "directions" are therefore given in the hope that they may help the reader use the book profitably; it is entirely possible, of course, to achieve the same result by a different route. Nonetheless, they may be helpful.

SETTING OUR SIGHTS

To use a book properly, we should locate its aims. The next paragraphs alert the reader to what he may expect from this book.

First of all, this book is intended to promote a fresh and vital study of Acts. It is best used when it serves as an incentive to read Acts for one's self. If the act of reading this book *about* the Bible becomes a substitute for reading the Bible itself, the value of the book has been dissipated. Apart from its help in understanding Acts and its relevance for today's church life, this book has meager value, for it is neither a commentary nor a "history of early Christianity." For this reason it is written in a way that the reader must have a copy of the New Testament before him as he reads. Only then can the argument be followed with precision; moreover, only then can the reader check his own understanding of Acts against that of this book.

A second aim is to demonstrate a kind of Bible study which combines a close examination of the text[1] with a serious probing of issues raised by it. It is not enough simply to learn "what the Bible says." It is not even enough to learn what the biblical authors intended to say in their own times, though this minimum is absolutely essential. Rather, Bible study in depth becomes possible only if we ask serious questions about what we read. Through these we probe the underlying meaning, and thus take the risk of discovering that there is a significant disagreement between the text and ourselves over the truth of the matter. The person who has never experienced this tension with the text ought to ask whether his real self has yet heard the real message of the Bible.

There is a far-reaching theological reason for this: Insofar as the Bible is a means by which God makes himself known to readers who live between Eden and Heaven (that is, in history), the Word of God encounters resistance. Hence we ought not to be surprised if we find ourselves wanting to argue with the author of Acts. Encountering the meaning of Acts on this level is essential if one wants to do more than inform himself about a piece of ancient Christian literature. Going beyond simply learning *about* Acts to the point where one must actually *reckon with* Acts is an important element of reading the Bible as Scripture. In other words, Bible study can be vital if one not only asks what the Bible says, but whether this is true, true enough to believe, believe deeply enough to act on. For example, what difference does it make what Acts says about the life of the church? Until one is willing to reckon seriously with it, what Acts says about the church is only a more or less interesting detail in the history of ideas. The only way the reader will really know whether the Bible is relevant is by asking whether he can believe it enough to stand with it. Asking this question openly and trying hard to answer it honestly (and this means allowing people to say "No" to what Acts says) will do much to vitalize Bible study in today's church.

Third, because this book does not simply digest what Acts says but discusses the issues it presents, the book is also a primer in thinking about the Christian faith and the church. In this sense, it is a kind of elemental "Biblical Theology" — a somewhat systematic exploration of the meaning of Acts. Therefore it is to be studied and pondered, not simply skimmed and outlined. And yet it certainly is not a complete statement of biblical faith, neither in detail nor in scope. It will not even deal with the entire book of Acts, let alone the whole New Testament. We shall examine five sections or slices of Acts. Many important matters will necessarily be ignored. On any given topic, a complete understanding of the New Testament would take us far beyond Acts to the other books. What we will lose in breadth, however, we hope to gain in depth. Behind this policy lies the conviction that it is better to examine carefully a limited number of passages than to pile generality upon generality. "Covering the whole subject" often means smothering it.

Finally, because the kind of Bible study this book offers must take place within the church, where one interpreter faces another, this book combines analyses of Acts with the author's personal understanding of what Acts means today. Moreover, because the book will be used largely by study groups, it does not hesitate to oversimplify issues in order to provoke thought and to elicit discussion. The value of the book should not be measured simply by the number of times the reader can scribble "Amen!" in the margins, but by the number of times he may put question marks or "No." The occasions for dissent are there not because the author wants to pick a fight with the reader but in order to call forth a deeper conversation about the meaning of the text. Furthermore, the book has been written in ordinary (and sometimes colloquial) language not simply because it is designed for general use throughout the churches, but because the issues themselves demand it. Increasingly, the suspicion arises that much of the jargon used in churches is actually a way of avoiding embarrassing questions — that the words we love best are often more a smoke screen behind which we can hide our confusion than a means of saying what we really think. It makes little difference whether this be the jargon of current existentialist Christianity, sophisticated fundamentalism under the banner of "evangelicalism," or an earlier American liberalism. Each has learned to hide behind its pet phrases. Therefore this book interprets Acts as directly as possible in order to generate a three-way conversation among the author of Acts, all his readers (ancient and modern alike), and the writer of this volume.

SUGGESTED STEPS FOR STUDY

1. Obviously, the place to begin is with the Book of Acts itself, all of it. It should be read through, preferably at one sitting and more than one reading. The total wealth of detail in such a book cannot be kept in mind, nor should one try to absorb all of it at once. A reading of the whole book, however, should have two goals in mind:

(a) *A sense of what the Book of Acts is about and where it is going.* One way to get at this is to observe not simply what it reports but what it leaves out (for example, information about how Christianity got to Rome). A second way to get hold of the book as a whole is to make a rough outline showing the major divisions. All commentaries do this (so does Chapter 1 of this book), but it is very important that the reader should try to do it for himself.

(b) *The discovery of what the writer's main concerns are.* The next chapter will do some of this investigation too, but the reader should test what is said there and add to it from his own study.

2. As the next step, one should read the passages in Acts with which the chapters of this book deal. These should be studied in more detail; each chapter begins with a guide to the text of Acts. At this stage, it is important to begin combining a detailed study of the text with one's own questions about it and its relevance. That is, the reader should ask two questions: First, what *did* the writer want to say? (What did it mean to his first readers?) Then he is prepared to ask, What *does* his writing say now? (What does it mean to me?) It is of fundamental importance that the reader begin to develop his ability to ask both questions and to learn to live with the answers.

3. After the reader has made his own effort to understand Acts, he is ready to read the bulk of this book. This volume is not the Answer Book to Acts, but one man's attempt to hear clearly enough what the writer has said to his first readers to allow him to speak to us also.

4. One should go back to Acts again, and give the writer another chance to say something we missed before. Now is also the time to read other parts of the Bible, for in most cases even the familiar passages will look somewhat different after one has lived with Acts for a while.

This is about as far as one can guide a reader in advance, because if he is receptive and the Spirit is willing, no one can predict just what will or should happen next, except to point out that study alone cannot go on forever. Sooner or later, insight should galvanize into conviction, and conviction into action. Did not Jesus remind an enthusiastic listener, "Blessed are they who hear the Word of God — and keep it"?

CHAPTER ONE

APPROACHING THE BOOK OF ACTS

These things happened to them . . . but they were written down for our instruction, upon whom the end of the ages has come.
—St. Paul (1 Corinthians 10:11)

*We are living in an era of severe divine judgment; but for that very reason, in an era of divine grace and promise.**
—Joseph L. Hromadka

*. . . the Bible will give little comfort to either the pessimist or the optimist. Against the pessimist the interpreter of the Bible must hold that God, and not the devil, is now at work in our history. Against the optimist, it must be said that our history is not yet fulfilled. . . .***
—Fred J. Denbeaux

APPROACHING
THE BOOK OF ACTS

TODAY, THE CHURCH LIVES IN THE WORLD WITHOUT CHRISTENDOM.
This situation is so radically different from what we have
known and come to regard as normal that many Christians
have not yet grasped its consequences. It is necessary, therefore, to note the situation of the church within which we are
studying Acts.

WHERE WE READ ACTS

By "Christendom" we mean a Christian society, one which
not only is based on Christianity historically (as are Europe
and America) but one which is basically Christian in its
values, its ways of thinking, its artistic expression, its aims for
the future. There is no doubt that such a Christendom once
existed in Europe.[1] In fact, "Christendom" used to be a way
of talking about European civilization, of which America is
an extension. Today, the North Atlantic community can no
longer be regarded as Christendom.

Christendom died in 1914. In that fateful summer, Christian nations began a barbaric war which destroyed the last
shreds of the old Christian Europe (the French Revolution
had been a signal of what was to come). Not only did Holy
Russia become anti-Christian, but the adjusted Christianity of
Christendom was too weak to meet the crises that followed
World War I. The successful rise of Fascism and Nazism

17

showed how superficial Christianity had become and that Christendom's church was incapable of dealing with the sharp alternative these political faiths presented. The few individual Christians who resisted Hitler stand out in contrast against virtually the whole church which trooped to his colors.

This is not simply the problem of "tired old Europe." In America, which has been predominantly Protestant, we find ourselves moving into a post-Protestant period. The time when Protestant Christianity set the pace for the United States as a whole is past, though in some sections (such as the southeastern quarter) this trend is not yet so apparent as elsewhere. The white Protestant used to manage this country and tolerate the Jews, Mormons, Catholics, and freethinkers as long as they "kept their place." Now these minorities are saying that "their place" is precisely the same as his place. We have had a Catholic president; we have Jews and Mormons in responsible public office, as well as persons with no conscious religious affiliation at all. Though Protestants still form the largest bulk of the population, the United States is no longer the Protestant nation it was two generations ago.

Actually, we have never been as Christian (and therefore as Protestant) as we pretend. A Protestant minority in league with rationalists and non-religious pragmatists shaped what we call the American Way of Life. But today the shape of American life is less and less in the hands of Christian influences, and still less in the hands of Protestants. Some may regard this change as disaster. Actually, it means we are rapidly becoming the democracy we have been trumpeting about. To be precise, we have discovered that democracy in a land such as ours, with its mixture of races and religions, has brought us pluralism.

Pluralism means that there is more than one interpretation of life which is shaping society — not just the Protestant Christian, but many others besides. It means that we must now reckon with the fact that the American Way of Life in the future will be some sort of compromise among these competing ideas about what American society should be like.[2] In short, Americans are not only in a post-Christian situation but in a specifically post-Protestant one.[3]

In addition we see that all religious interpretations of life face an even more radical alternative — a basically non-religious understanding of human life and society. This goes under various names. With regard to traditional religious patterns, it is often called secularism; with regard to theories about man it can be labeled naturalism; with regard to ethics it can be dubbed humanistic pragmatism. In any case, those who have this outlook contend that society can be organized and the nature and destiny of man interpreted without reference to God at all. This is not an anti-religious, anti-God movement because it does not regard religion or God as worth fighting any longer. In fact, this view simply bypasses God altogether and regards the whole idea of religion as being as outdated as a hitching-post.[4]

We are therefore in a somewhat comical situation. We see various kinds of religious and denominational groups competing with one another for the franchise to service the American society, while a large segment of that society has already shown that it doesn't want that service from any of them, any more than it wants blacksmiths. For this reason, Paul Ramsey has said that ours is the first attempt in the history of man "to build a culture upon the premise that God is dead."[5] In this light, congregations contain people who are paying their respects to a departed Power and wonder what it must have been like when God was still alive and at work. Someone has observed that, in this situation, the true believer is the man who misses God.

In other words, the Christian church finds itself more and more a stranger in the lands which it has called home for centuries. Even in America, where it has enjoyed its greatest outward success, the church is becoming more and more incapable of shaping national life.[6] The fact that many churches are full may not be a sign that the church is strong so much as a mark of spiritual hunger among overfed churchmen. To be sure, anyone can think of dozens of exceptions, but the very fact that these are *exceptions* stresses the rule. The rule, if we may speak of such, is that today the churches are full, silent, and often unimportant in the life of the community. And most people could hardly care less.

READING ACTS IN TODAY'S CHURCH

But what has all this to do with studying Acts? Precisely this: The church which reads Acts today lives in this kind of situation. Unless our reading of Acts is to be merely a pious escape from the facts, it is virtually as important to know our own situation as to know what we are reading. When we study the book of Acts in the church today, we do not enter a decompression chamber from which the pressures of the outside world are removed so that we may meditate in tranquillity. To the contrary, when we rightly assess the situation of the church in today's world, we are in a position to read Acts with penetration and vitality. Because the reasons behind this assertion may not be apparent, let us consider briefly what it means to read Acts as Scripture (see also "How to Use This Book").

The art of reading the Bible as Scripture centers in the ability to penetrate the text to the point where we can converse with the writers. We bring our questions to the text, and they present their witness to us. Because it is not always easy to hear what these writers have to say, our reading may require more concentration than we are prepared to give. But when there is a real meeting between writer and reader, the reader often finds himself led to reexamine his own situation and to renew his convictions. He may also discover a new power for action. Theologians call this the work of the Holy Spirit. There is no way of guaranteeing, of course, that this penetration will occur. But reading Acts as Scripture means reading it while reckoning with the possibility that it will.

Of course, there are other ways of reading Acts. One is to analyze it scientifically, the way scholars work on the Dead Sea Scrolls, and to stop when the author's intent and product are understood. Such scientific work is absolutely necessary if one wants to know what the Scrolls actually say and mean. In exactly the same way, scientific study of the Bible is necessary if we are to know precisely what it contains, why the author wrote it, and what he intended to say. The point is not whether we shall pursue this kind of Bible study, but whether we shall continue to search after we have answered these questions. Reading the Bible as Scripture, in the sense sketched above, means going beyond informed reading. It means using everything we can find out about the Bible in order to prepare us to take seriously what the writer has to say. In other words, we shall not be content to observe how the writer addressed his first readers, but shall try to enter into conversation with him ourselves. We shall be bystanders long enough to learn how to join the first readers in hearing what the author has to say.[7]

The implication is clear. Since that author's meaning is anchored to the situation in which he confronts his first readers, and since our understanding of what he wrote is anchored to the situation in which we read, the more we have in common with his situation the easier it is for him to speak directly to us. In light of what we have pointed out about the church today, we may state our thesis this way: The church today is closer to the situation of Acts than it has been in almost 1600 years. The church in his day, as in ours, lived in a world without Christendom. The church, then as now, was living in a frontier situation. This new fact about our times makes it possible for us to understand with freshness the acts of those apostles in our kind of church.

We must not overlook an important difference, however.

While both the writer of Acts and the modern reader live in a world without Christendom, we live on this side of a Christendom that once existed. This means we look back on experiences of the church which the author could not anticipate. He could not foresee what Christianity would become, but we look back on what it has been. It is precisely this difference that generates the kinds of questions we put to the writer, for in our situation we cannot avoid asking whether the writer of Acts is right about his vision of the church in the world. In other words, it is largely the difference in our situations that creates the dialogue between ourselves as modern readers and the Book of Acts. Before that dialogue can occur, we need to become acquainted with the writer and his book.

THE BOOK OF ACTS AS A WHOLE

We must see the Book of Acts as a whole even though we shall not study the whole of Acts. It is necessary to see how the sections we study are related to the whole book.

Seen as part of the New Testament as a whole, Acts is clearly a unique book, for it is the only one which narrates the work of the church as the sequel to the work of Jesus. Acts begins by referring to "the first book" in which the mission of Jesus had been told (1:1). Thus Acts is Volume Two of a two-volume set; the Gospel According to Luke is Volume One.[8]

The content of Acts is unique in three ways:

1. Though Acts tells the story of the early church, it is both more than a history and less than a history. It is more in that the author wants to do more than report what happened; he wants to show why it happened. This "why" is not simply an historical cause, the kind we speak of when we say that the slavery controversy was a cause of the American Civil War. This author sees the real cause of the events as the purposes of God. A book which tells history as the working-out of God's purposes is thus more than a history book—it is at the same time a theology book.

Acts is also less than a history book because there is a great deal of the history of the early church which the author does not tell. For example, he is completely silent about how Christianity got to Egypt or Rome. Even more intriguing are the things he leaves out of the stories of Paul. For example, he never says that Paul had any trouble with the churches he founded, yet Paul's own letters show he was frequently embroiled in controversies with them. The fact that all such problems are left out of the story shows that Acts is less than "a history of the early church." It is not like a complete film of a football game, but like the yearbook which prints selected snapshots of important games. The selection is presented as the unfolding of God's purposes through the work of the apostles, chiefly Paul.

2. Acts includes a great variety of materials. Especially important are the speeches and sermons. We are tempted to conclude that the "acts" of the apostles consisted largely of their talks! Besides, there are miracle stories, reports of hearings before judges and governors, a summary of the first church council, a missionary travelogue, and the story of a sea voyage climaxed by a shipwreck and a snake-bite. When we remember that our author left out many things of interest to us, we conclude he probably had definite reasons for including what he did. An important step in understanding Acts is locating these reasons.

3. Though the book is now called "The Acts of the Apostles," it is really concerned with only two of the apostles, Peter and Paul. This concentration on these two is all the more intriguing because the book opens with a story of how Matthias was elected to replace Judas Iscariot so that there would be twelve apostles again. Yet, "the twelve" are mentioned only once more (at 6:2), and as individuals they are ignored completely. Acts is not a twelve-cylinder account of the apostolic church, but the story of the church told through the careers of two men, Peter and Paul, especially Paul.

Thus the Book of Acts is a piece of historical writing that is not really a "history"; it contains an assortment of material and yet is not an early Christian anthology of short stories; it is a narrative centering in the careers of two men and yet is not a biography of either one. Acts is unique. Our next step is to detect the writer's reasons for producing such a document.

THE STORY BEHIND LUKE-ACTS

The story which we shall piece together results from years of detective work carried on by many sleuths (in this case, the biblical scholars). The case, however, has not yet been solved completely. It may never be, because there are no eye-witnesses to whom we can go to check our conclusions.

Detective stories are commonly called "whodunits" because their central problem is the identity of the criminal. The same is true of Luke-Acts, for a primary problem is, Who wrote it? Unfortunately, the author never identifies himself. The tradition of the church has, however, named the writer: Luke, the physician whom Paul mentions in Colossians 4:14 and Philemon 24. It is almost impossible to verify this tradition. Paul never says Luke was an author as well as a doctor, and Acts contains no points of contact whatever with anything said in Colossians and Philemon, except that Paul was in prison. This means that whoever wants to test the traditional identification of the author must do so by drawing conclusions from a wide assortment of facts. Just at this point, however, investigators have failed completely to reach an agreement.[9]

We cannot, of course, present the complex web of arguments, but we can look briefly at important evidence. At several places the narrative shifts from "they" to "we": Acts 16:10-17; 20:5-16; 21:1-18; 27:1-28:16. From this fact we draw two important conclusions. (1) Since there is no change of style in these sections, we may regard the author of the "we" sections as the author of the passages between the "we" sections. (2) Since the "we" sections report stories of Paul, we conclude that the writer of Acts was with Paul at least some of the time.[10] For the information he has about the period before Paul, he clearly depends on some sort of tradition as he does for the stories of Jesus (note Luke 1:1-4). Thus, while we know a good deal about this man, we still do not know for sure whether his name was Luke, nor whether he was a physician.[11] In short, the tradition has not been proved or disproved by literary analysis.

The most serious objections to the traditional identification of the author center in his portrait of Paul. Many scholars are simply not convinced that a traveling companion of Paul's would have said what he did about Paul (*e.g.*, that Paul would refer to the witnesses of Jesus' resurrection without including himself; compare Acts 13:30-31 with 1 Corinthians 15:3-11). We shall return to these questions.

In this book, we shall regard Luke as the author, knowing that there are serious problems connected with this tradition. Actually, our understanding of Acts depends more on the author's motive and method than it does on his name. As in the detective story, the case is not solved until the motive is related to the deed. This is our next task.

To understand the aim of the writer, we begin with the circumstances in which he wrote. Basically, we note that in Luke's time[12] the church, now an institution alongside the synagogue, was under increasing pressures from within and without. Three aspects of this situation, in particular, generated problems:

1. By the time Luke wrote, the church had grown from a small group of Palestinian Jews who believed in Jesus, to an international, multilingual, interracial institution. This church consisted of a family of congregations found in virtually all important cities east of Rome. The church was getting old enough to have a history of its own, even though in the past it had not expected to have a history at all. The earliest believers had expected the Second Coming of Christ "almost any

day now," certainly within the lifetime of Paul. Moreover, it was commonly believed that the Return would be part of the final drama of history, a convulsion in which the anti-God forces would be galvanized into action against the saints. By the time Acts was written, three occasions had come and gone when such a climax was expected. The first occurred in A.D. 41, when the mad emperor Caligula tried to have his statue erected in the Jerusalem temple. Reading the Book of Daniel in the light of this event led many to think that the end was at hand. Next, Nero had persecuted the Christians in Rome and had martyred Peter and Paul along with the others. Third, when the Jews revolted against the Romans in A.D. 66, the insurrection was climaxed by a long siege (in A.D. 70) and fierce brutality.

These horrible experiences came and went, but the Lord stayed away and the church lived on. A fundamental question emerged: What was the meaning of the church's hope in the light of this kind of history? What was the meaning of the fact that the church had a history at all, inasmuch as it looked for the end of all history? What was the meaning of the fact that instead of a returned Messiah reigning in Jerusalem there was now a world-wide church? Luke wrote with these problems in mind.

2. The church had left the synagogue which had been its first home. The earliest Christians were all Jews, but by the time Luke wrote, important changes had occurred; the church was more and more Gentile, and the Jews themselves had rejected the gospel. At the same time, this predominantly Gentile church was using the synagogue's Bible (our Old Testament) as its Scripture, and was regarding itself as the true inheritor of the place of Israel in God's purpose.

This main-line development was not without conflicts, for there were many who wanted to repudiate the Old Testament heritage. In other words, evangelizing the Gentiles produced a struggle for the proper understanding of what the church and its message really were. Inevitably, this struggle involved a struggle for leadership of the churches, as writings like 3 John show.[18] The final outcome did not become clear until years after Acts was written, but the beginnings of the pattern are visible in Acts, suggesting that the right doctrine is to be found in the duly constituted leadership of the church, from Jerusalem forward. The doctrinal controversies, which involved much more than the problem of the Old Testament, made clear the need for authoritative guidelines to proper beliefs and for authoritative interpreters. The result was that the bishops were accepted as the definitive interpreters of the creeds. Acts seems to stand at the beginning of this development.

3. The Roman government was a third factor in Luke's situation. By this time, at least one congregation (Rome) had seen its members die for the faith. When Acts was written, the Roman persecution was past, but the precedent had been set and new pressures were on the horizon. In a few years, the church would face a drive to compel all citizens to show they were loyal citizens of Rome by confessing publicly that the emperor personified divine power. As a result, Acts insists that the church is not subversive.

In a word, then, these three factors shaped Luke's aims as he wrote Acts: the fact of the church in history, the problems which emerged as the church left the synagogue, and the pressures of the state. Luke does not provide footnotes to show how he dealt with each issue. The sensitive interpreter will, however, be alert to see these factors at work. At the beginning of Volume One, Luke told Theophilus[14] that he was writing in order "that you may know the truth concerning the things of which you have been informed." That is, he is providing an account of Jesus and the church to help Theophilus see who Jesus was and what the church is. We may assume competing interpretations were available. Luke wanted to provide a definitive account in light of these three factors.

We can only sketch in barest outline his method and re-sources. Luke is one of the few writers of the New Testament who admits he used sources (Luke 1:1-4) ; probably some were documents and others were stories circulating by word of mouth. Locating the sources of Acts is an infinitely complex task which has not yet been done satisfactorily. We can make a few educated guesses, however. We have already mentioned the "we" source. To this Luke added a variety of material: stories of events such as the conversion of Paul, traditions of what the apostles' preaching had been like (a special problem to be discussed in Chapter 3), his own threading together of the stories into a running narrative. We have no reason to think he told everything he knew, or that he wrote it down exactly as he heard it without shaping it to fit his aims. It is much more likely that he brought all this material together into a story which he believed could speak to the church of his own day. Our final step is to survey the results of his work.

THE PANORAMA OF ACTS

The Book of Acts begins the story in the days immediately after Easter, and ends two years after Paul arrived in Rome as a prisoner, a period roughly between A.D. 30 and 60. A bird's-eye view will suffice to give a sweep of the whole.

The book can be divided into three major parts: 1:6-9:31; 9:32-19:20; 19:21-28:31.[15] Part One (1:6-9:31) begins after the Ascension of Jesus. A few days later, during the Jewish festival of Pentecost, the brethren experience the Holy Spirit in a way that enables them to launch their public mission. The group grows rapidly, lives together communally, and enjoys some popular support but is subjected to official pressure at the same time. Soon the group has two elements, a conservative group clinging to the traditional customs of Judaism and a liberal wing which lives in Greek style. One of the leaders of the latter, Stephen, is arrested for criticizing the temple and stoned to death. This event touches off a campaign of persecution led by Paul of Tarsus; the refugees become propagators of the new faith. When Paul is converted, the stage is set for the transformation of the church through the conversion of the Gentiles.

Part Two (9:32-19:20) opens with Peter at the seacoast, where a Roman army officer is converted and stays in his house. Luke sees this as a precedent for converting the Gentiles. Beginning with Chapter 13, Paul moves to the center of the story, and dominates the rest of the book. It is he who makes Peter's precedent into a principle, as he begins a series of campaigns to convert Gentiles. When Paul's work meets resistance from the Jerusalem conservatives, it becomes necessary to call a council to settle the matter. The session ends in a compromise slanted toward Paul, which clears the air for him to continue his work. This reaches its climax when he sees that his work in Asia Minor and Greece is accomplished. The actual narrative of his work consists mostly of short stories about his experiences.

Part Three (19:21-28:31) is dominated by the end of Paul's career. The first section is concerned with his going to Jerusalem and his arrest there. The second concerns his efforts to defend himself and the appeal for a final verdict from Caesar himself. This appeal takes him to Rome, though as a prisoner and not as a free apostle. Here the story ends. Not a word is said about Paul's trial or its outcome. The implication all along has been that he would not be released (see, for example, 20:17-38).[16] Tradition outside the New Testament holds that he was beheaded during the orgy unleashed by Nero in A.D. 64. There is no valid reason to deny this.

The chapters which follow assume that Luke's work is worth studying and that his message is worth hearing today. After all, he tells about that earlier era when the church was sent to bear witness in a world which, like ours, was without Christendom. Perhaps he has a word for us in our time.

WITNESS WITH POWER

And there appeared to them tongues as of fire. . . . And they were all filled with the Holy Spirit. . . .

—ST. LUKE (Acts 2:3, 4)

Without this fire, religion is dead ashes.
—JOHN S. WHALE

No ecclesiastical institution, no organized church effort . . . is a remedy against this new secularism. No artificially preserved religious institutions can possibly help. . . . The real, challenging question is: How can the church be a real transforming power, something much more than a beautiful decoration of life? What ought we, Christians, to do? *

—JOSEPH L. HROMADKA

TEXT OF ACTS: Acts 1:1-2:42

THINGS TO LOOK FOR:

1. First, notice the overall structure of these chapters:
   A. Introduction (1:1-5)
   B. Promise and preparation
      1. Commissioned (1:6-11)
      2. The original group (1:12-14)
      3. Twelve again (1:15-26)
   C. The promised power
      1. When the spirit came (2:1-13)
      2. Christian preaching (2:14-36)
      3. The response (2:37-42)

2. Luke is the only New Testament writer to speak of forty days between Easter and Ascension, and he does this only in Acts. Luke 24:50-53 does not hint it.[1] Note the way the other gospels end. (Mark 16:9-20 was added later, after the original ending was lost. No one knows how this gospel originally ended.) What is the promise Jesus makes? Why are the disciples to remain in Jerusalem? In Matthew and Mark, they are told to go to Galilee; in John they go without Jesus' command.

3. Why do the disciples replace Judas? What concept of the church is revealed by this step?

4. Peter's sermon will be discussed later. Notice, however, that the appeal centers in a plea for repentance and the promise of baptism and the Spirit. What is repentance? Why did the early Christians baptize? Nowhere in Luke's writings do we read that Jesus commanded them to do this. The risen Lord gives this command in Matthew's gospel (28:19), but Luke probably did not know Matthew.

5. The coming of the Spirit is told differently in John 20:19-28. Also, Paul assumes that all Christians have the Spirit, but never says anything about Pentecost. See Romans 8:1-17, 26-27; 1 Corinthians 12:4-13.

6. What are the major questions you have about the Holy Spirit? What does Luke want to say about the Spirit?

CHAPTER TWO

WITNESS WITH POWER

THE BOOK OF ACTS BEGINS THE STORY OF THE CHURCH WITH a question, "Lord, will you at this time restore the kingdom to Israel?" (1:6). This was a natural question. Jesus' resurrection had revealed him to be the Messiah, the Christ.[2] We easily forget the original meaning of the word, for we are accustomed to think that the name "Christ" means "a divine savior from sin." Actually, this is not its original meaning but a reinterpretation made by Christians in the light of Jesus.

PROMISE AND PREPARATION

Originally, and in Jesus' day, the Jews expected a Messiah whom God would bring on the scene at the Last Day to liberate his people, gather the dispersed Jews, and rule in God's name. This messianic kingdom was to fulfill the ancient promises God had made to the Jewish people, beginning with Abraham (see Genesis 12). In other words, "messiah" was not simply a religious title but a political one as well. To the ancient Jew, a non-political messiah was about as conceivable as a non-military general or a non-liturgical priest.

In this light, the disciples' question made sense. Since they believed Jesus was the Messiah, they expected him to begin the Messiah's work. Besides, Jesus had promised that they would sit on twelve thrones, judging twelve tribes — a symbolic way of promising them places of prominence in the kingdom (Luke 22:28-30). They were eager to take office as the bureaucrats of the kingdom of God.

In a significant way, their question is our question too. We ask it with different words, of course. We ask it when we yearn for Christendom, when we seek political power for the church. We press this question whenever we itch to manage the world in the name of God. This question, in some form, lurks behind the attempt to establish the kingdom of God in America. It is behind the scenes in maneuvers to get legislatures to make public laws out of Protestant pietism's attitudes toward Sunday and whiskey.[8] It is woven into many attempts to turn the kingdoms of this world into the kingdom of our Christ by power politics and pressure-group tactics alone.

We must be clear: The question is not whether the church should participate in public affairs; nor whether it should use the instruments of social change (such as power structures in finance) to advance the cause of justice. The idea that "only changed hearts will change social structures" is far too simple to be helpful; the reverse is equally clear, that changes in society change men's hearts. Attitudes toward desegregation, for example, have been changed more since the Supreme Court decision of 1954 than before. What is at stake is the *basis and aim* of the church's participation in public life and the way it understands both its involvement and its instruments.

Jesus' reply points us to a basis for social action which we are as little prepared to accept as the first disciples, and we are as disappointed and as offended as they were: "It is not for you to know times or seasons which the Father has fixed by his own authority. But you shall receive power when the Holy Spirit has come upon you; and you shall be my witnesses . . ." (1:7f.).

There are three elements of this reply which merit attention:

1. The church is not supposed to worry about the schedule

of history. This answer was important in Luke's day because the church was beginning to wonder about the Second Coming, just as we are concerned about the future of the church in a world without Christendom. Already in New Testament times, men began asking the question which is phrased, "Where is the promise of his coming? For, ever since the fathers fell asleep [died], all things have continued as they were from the beginning of creation" (2 Peter 3:4). In other words, Christians then were concerned about when the goal of history would be reached (or, more precisely, when history would be replaced by what the Second Coming was to bring). Even if many Christians today are not nervous about the Second Coming, they have basically the same issue in mind when they wonder about the future of the church and begin to have second thoughts about the reality of its message. But Acts rejects all efforts to guess the time of the Second Coming — that is, the time when the tension between what we believe and what we see around us will be resolved. Acts offers instead something more important than worrying whether history is on schedule or not. People who connect the morning paper with Daniel and Revelation may find themselves arguing with Luke when they insist that it *is* their business to "break the code" of God's schedule. In the same way, Christian strategists who plan the work of the church with a view toward controlling world affairs for Jesus are likewise embarrassed by this text. Still, it is part of Scripture and we must come to terms with it.

2. The church will receive power. Power is precisely what the disciples wanted, and it is what we want too. Like the first followers we would love to be the administrators of God's will on earth. But Jesus does not promise this kind of power. The kind of power he talks about does not come from being installed in an office with a staff of secretaries and an expense account. Nor is it simply a religious word for sheer executive authority. The power Jesus had in mind is clear.

3. Jesus promised power to be witnesses in the world. No more and no less. The whole book of Acts is built around this theme. As we shall see in the next chapter, this witness-work centers in the resurrection and its meaning.

In other words, instead of being assigned the responsibility of managing Christendom, the church is given a mandate to be a living witness to the resurrection. This is why the decay of Christendom can free the church to go about its task — if it has the courage to accept it.

With Jesus' words ringing in their ears, the disciples saw him for the last time and returned to Jerusalem to order their common life together.

The story of the election of Matthias (1:15-26) is important because it discloses that the church believed it must have twelve apostles, even though it would not have a twelve-member cabinet to administer the world for God. This is an important conviction. Having been promised power to witness in the world during the absence of the Messiah (between his departure and return), the church found itself to be an interim institution, a kind of temporary substitute for the kingdom of God. Insofar as it can bear witness to the meaning of Jesus, it is also the place where the kingdom of God now has at least token reality.

At the same time, the idea of needing twelve apostles shows that the church thought of itself as Israel, for the twelve symbolize the traditional twelve tribes. Here we see an important point. Ten of these tribes had disappeared from history 750 years before, the so-called "lost tribes of Israel." However, it was a standard feature of Jewish hope that, in the End-time, all Israel would be reconstituted and reunited. This would include not simply all Jews scattered throughout the world at the time but also the so-called "lost tribes" which had been absorbed into the peoples of the ancient Near East. Therefore, when the church insisted that it must have twelve apostles, it claimed, in a symbolic way, to be this Final Israel, the goal of God's purpose for his people. At the same time, because the Messiah was not here to rule over them but would return, the church was really an Israel-in-waiting, an Israel-in-the-making. Even after the church became largely Gentile, it kept the Old Testament because of the conviction that the church was the true Israel of God. Wherever it remembers this identification seriously, there is no place for anti-Semitism.

One more point must be seen: The Christian witness to the resurrection of Jesus cannot be separated from the witness to the meaning of the church. We will touch on this principle again. Here we simply note that the church is not basically a promotional group organized to talk about Easter. What the group believes about Jesus and what it believes about itself cannot be split apart. This is because whoever believes that Jesus is the Messiah identifies himself with the Messiah's people. There can be no Messiah without a messianic community, any more than there can be a general without an army or a king without a kingdom. The church is the messianic community because it believes God's Messiah is Jesus. Conversely, only this community believes Jesus is the Messiah. In short, whoever believes that God raised Jesus and made him the Messiah admits that he, the believer, is a member of the community of faith that knows this fact.

The inference is clear. There can be no vital witness to the gospel by timid Christians who have an inferiority complex about the church. The word "church" here does not refer simply to the organization (which does embarrass us) but to the company of believers, some of whom are not found on membership lists at all. Unfortunately, the palsy of modern congregations is often more real to us than the power of God in the resurrection. However, this fact does not change the logic of the situation.

We are not the first believers who have felt powerless in the world. The same thing was true of First Church, Jerusalem — until it was caught in a divine whirlwind.

WHEN THE SPIRIT CAME

The promise of power was fulfilled at Pentecost. The story in Acts can easily derail us into insoluble problems; therefore we must pay strict attention to what Luke wants to tell us. We must not let our preconceived ideas about pentecostalism and the Holy Spirit hamper us, nor must we be unduly curious about "what really happened." Luke is not interested in reporting how the Holy Spirit got there, but in what happened after the Spirit arrived. Therefore, Luke writes in symbols which point to the powerful presence of God.

Before we look at some details, it is important to ask why Luke told the story in the first place, since his purpose is the best clue to his reasons for telling it the way he does.

In Acts 2, the story of the Spirit's coming is followed by a sermon which inaugurates Christian preaching. This double event (Spirit and sermon) launches the church's witness-work. Luke had told of the beginning of Jesus' mission in the same way. After Jesus was baptized, he received the Holy Spirit (Luke 3:21f) and returned (after defeating temptations) to his hometown synagogue. There he preached on a passage from Isaiah beginning, "The Spirit of the Lord is upon me." The theme of the sermon was that this passage was fulfilled in him (Luke 4:16-30). The message laid down the program of his mission. In other words, Luke says that the work of Jesus and the work of the church are both impelled and empowered by the Spirit. The two-volume work of Luke might be titled "The Works of the Spirit in the Era of Fulfillment." By beginning Volume One with the story of the Spirit-empowered Jesus and Volume Two with the story of the Spirit-impelled church, Luke gives the readers the clue they need to understand properly the stories which follow. For Luke, the key to the work of Jesus and the church is the source of their power, the Spirit.

With this accent in mind, we can detect the emphases Luke

makes in his story of Pentecost. Notice how much he leaves unsaid: The sound was *like* that of wind, and what they saw looked *like* fiery tongues. We do not even know where this took place or how the populace learned of it. Moreover, it is not clear how the people knew the disciples were Galileans, nor are we told why these Jews should have known the local dialects of native peoples from the plateaus of Pakistan to the hills of Italy, nor why the disciples were thought to be drunk although their words were clearly understood. These and similar problems can jam the signals Luke is trying to send. We must listen to Luke closely.

The story in Acts 2 is not only related to that of Luke 4, but also to what was said in Acts 1 — the promise of power and the claim to be the true Israel. The story in Acts 2 fulfills both.

First, all the hearers were Jews. Even though they came from all sorts of places, Luke insists they were Jews[4] who moved to Jerusalem. He emphasizes this fact because he wants to insist that the mission of the church begins with the Jews — those scattered throughout the ancient world as well as to those in Palestine. According to verse 10, the hearers included Gentile converts to Judaism as well. Thus, the audience represented the whole Israel as it existed at the time. Having twelve apostles equipped the church to address all Israel with the news about Jesus; receiving the Spirit empowered it to begin.

Next, all those present understood in their own dialects. Actually, Greek or Aramaic would have been understood by virtually all of them, but this circumstance was not important to Luke. He was impressed with the fact that the Spirit did not simply enable disciples to talk, but made it possible for each one present to understand them in his own terms. The power of the Spirit thus brought the ability to be understood. We will come back to the problems of communication in Chapter 5. Here we simply point out that Acts insists that the primary work of the Spirit is to empower the witnesses to be understood and not simply to make them excited babblers.[5]

Now we may summarize what Luke has said: Instead of the disciples becoming the administrators of the restored Israel, they are to be the empowered witnesses to the resurrection of Jesus. Instead of the authority to govern the agencies of the kingdom, they will have power to communicate the gospel, first to Israel and then to all the world. They were to be a group of empowered witnesses who insisted that the state of affairs in the world was at best only half true because Jesus is really the Messiah and Lord, whether the world knows this or not. Their job was to make it known. In this light we note that the situation of the early church was remarkably like our own. Actually we should turn the sentence around. As the controlling power of Anglo-Saxon Protestantism in America declines, we draw closer to the situation of the New Testament than the church has been since the fourth century. Hence Acts can speak more directly to our situation. Like the Apostles, we are witnesses in a world without Christendom; in this situation, the mandate of Jesus and the power of the Spirit merit special attention and obedience. We can understand the mandate more clearly if we see how Luke understood the work of the Spirit.

We have already noted that what Luke says about the Spirit in Acts is related to what he says about the Spirit in his companion volume, the Gospel According to Luke. We may now note five aspects of Luke's idea of the Spirit in the church. By noting what Acts says, we are not necessarily suggesting that here we find the most adequate New Testament concept of the Spirit; rather, we are trying to locate what this one writer has to say on the subject before we consider the Spirit as such and the problems we may have at this point. As a matter of procedure, it is best first to hear what the author has to say before we take up our own problems:

1. The Spirit is associated with baptism. Actually Luke

does not have a fully consistent view as to what this association is. Sometimes he reports that people are baptized because they have already received the Spirit (Acts 10:44-48), sometimes that they receive the Spirit in connection with baptism (2:38), and sometimes merely that they are baptized — saying nothing about the Spirit at all (8:35-40). But, basically, Luke believes that the Spirit normally comes to a man in connection with baptism (9:17-19). Baptism thus marks entry into the life of the Spirit and entry into the church at the same time.

2. The Holy Spirit sometimes initiates policies in the church. This function is especially clear in Acts 13:1-12. Luke does not think everything Paul did or wanted to do was an act of the Spirit (see especially 16:6-7), but he is convinced that basic decisions are guided by the Spirit (note the outcome in 16:9-10). He also reports that the church council's compromise was a decision reached by the Spirit's guidance (15:22-29). For him, this was not simply a pious phrase used to cover up the maneuvering in the committee meeting.

3. Luke also reports that the church had prophets, men whose experiences of the Spirit somehow enabled them to foresee the future course of events. One forecast a famine (11:27-30); others foresaw the arrest of Paul if he insisted on going to Jerusalem (21:3-4, 7-12). But Luke says Paul went anyway because the Spirit had told him to go (19:21; 20:22).

4. The Spirit is also at work in the institutional structure of the church. Luke does not emphasize this function, but he does report that Paul told the elders at Ephesus that "the Holy Spirit has made you guardians" of the church (20:28).

5. Finally, Luke says that there were persons who were "full of the Holy Spirit." The first person of whom he says this is Jesus (Luke 4:1), but he says it also of the so-called deacons (Acts 6:3-6), especially one of them, Stephen (6:10; 7:55), and of Barnabas (11:24). For some reason, however, he never says this about Paul. Luke is the only writer in the New Testament to use this phrase, and he probably had in mind a

particularly clear manifestation of God's power in the life of a holy man.

This rapid survey shows that Luke conceived the life and work of the church to be guided and empowered by the Spirit. He also expressed this conviction by reporting incidents in which "the Lord" appeared: 9:1-5, 10-19; 18:9-11; 22:17-21; 23:11. For him, these were alternate ways of talking about divine guidance.[6]

We are tempted to idealize earliest Christianity and then dismiss it, for one of two reasons:

1. These early churches were led by the apostles who had been with Jesus and who were in Jerusalem at Pentecost. This relationship gives them special standing in the history of the church. Hence we are tempted to regard this period as so "special" that it cannot say anything to us at all. Nevertheless, a close reading of Acts shows that having the apostles as leaders did not mean that the church had no problems; even the apostles were not angels, but human beings with their own peculiar compounds of fear and faith. Hence, some of the ways in which they met the crises of their times may be relevant to us today.

2. The story of the beginning at Pentecost stretches our credulity. Those conscientious Christians today who simply cannot accept the Pentecost story as a literal account of what happened are tempted to set aside the whole story of the church in Acts. Hence it is necessary for them to ask whether they can accept what Luke *intended* to say even if they cannot accept his narrative literally. In other words, is there a way of understanding the Spirit in the church, a way which does not depend on the flames and winds of Pentecost? This book asserts that there is.

For contemporary Christians to take seriously what Luke tells about the Spirit means to think rigorously about what the Spirit is, and what it is not, in the life of the church. Just as we must not admire and then dismiss the early church, so we also should not decide to "go back" to it. Even though the disappearance of what we call Christendom has put us in a situation similar to that of Acts, there is one aspect of our situation which can never be the same: The earliest Christians had a contagious enthusiasm generated partly by their own vivid memories of Jesus (including his appearances to them) and partly by their keen expectation that the end of the world and the beginning of a transformed age was virtually upon them. We, however, look back on nineteen centuries of unfulfilled waiting marked not only by feats of heroism but also by crimes against humanity done by the church in Christ's name. This perspective makes many Christians not only cautious but even cynical about whether God's Spirit is at work in the sort of thing the church has turned out to be.

Because we cannot ignore these nineteen centuries, it is *impossible* for us to "go back to Acts." Historically, it is always impossible to recreate an earlier period (unless one wants to do so for curiosity or entertainment as in Colonial Williamsburg, Va.). Theologically, it is *illegitimate* to try to do this, because God calls us to obedience in our own century and not in some golden age of the past; besides, such an effort to "go back" is really an effort to "force God's hand" so he will give us a duplicate Pentecost today.

Though we may neither dismiss nor imitate the first congregation, we may think constructively about what the Holy Spirit in the church *can* mean today. To do so, we must go beyond what Acts has to say, as we take note of the insights of Paul and John. The kinds of problems we face require the resources of the whole New Testament.

THE SPIRIT AND THE CHURCH

Today the church is embarrassed by the Holy Spirit. Usually it does not even want to discuss the subject. Because some Christians love to talk freely about the Holy Spirit, or "let themselves go" in holy excitement, the rest of us prefer to avoid talking altogether about the Holy Spirit lest we get tarred by the same brush.

The church is also afraid of the Spirit. From time to time, pentecostalism has seized the church. Each time, this movement has brought vigorous (and sometimes violent) criticism upon the traditional church and a disruption of its life. The church has defended itself by saying that the true and proper place for the Spirit to work is within the institutional church itself, in the work of its bishops, presidents, and executive committees. One could write the history of the church as the story of its effort to domesticate the Spirit of God into the unseen power of church leadership. Paul once reminded the Corinthians (2 Corinthians 3:17) that where the Spirit of the Lord is, there is freedom. Few things terrorize institutions so much as freedom exercised in the name of God, because this threatens to undermine the authority of the officers. In some ways, the church fears the Spirit (or, more precisely, men claiming the Spirit) working freely within the church, as much as storms raging on the outside.

Moreover, the church does not know how to think of the Spirit. This is one reason we have such difficulty in dealing with people who claim the Spirit's power. We simply do not know what to make of the phrase "the Holy Spirit" or "the Holy Ghost." Some people may suspect that the Holy Ghost is some sort of sacred spook! We do not even know whether we should speak of the Spirit of God as "he" or "it."[7] More important, we are not at all sure whether we are talking about an impersonal force, such as pressure, or a personal presence.

Our task is laid out: first to clarify what we mean by "the Holy Spirit," then to look at our own congregational life.

To understand what we are doing when we discuss the Holy Spirit, we must say two preliminary things:

1. It is not possible to make a definition of the Holy Spirit. Definitions mark off the limits, set the boundaries of meaning. But, in Christian theology, the Holy Spirit is one element of

the Trinity; therefore talking about the Holy Spirit is talking about God. God cannot be defined, because no human being can set the boundaries of God. Moreover, the Spirit is by nature free, even free from human definitions. What can we do, then? If we cannot define the Holy Spirit, we can unsnarl our words so that we can think straight. If we keep this purpose in mind, we can make momentary definitions to point us in the right direction. But if we slip into thinking that such definitions tell us exactly what the Spirit is, we are simply carving idols with words.

2. Talking about the Holy Spirit is a distinctive (and somewhat dangerous) way of talking about God and human experience at the same time. Everything we know about the Spirit of God comes through human experience. The experience of the Spirit is the experience of man with God. Therefore, whenever we discuss the Holy Spirit, we aim to interpret our most profound experiences of God. In this way each person contributes to our common understanding of the Spirit. At the same time, it must be pointed out that there is no way anyone can prove that a particular experience is an experience of God, whether this be a feeling of reverence, an ecstatic moment, or a sober insight. Because the Spirit is "part" of the Trinity, one can no more prove that the Spirit is present, or that a particular experience results from his power, than one can prove that God exists. In other words, all talk about the Holy Spirit is a confession, a belief-ful way of understanding ourselves and God. This is why the history of the church presents us with what looks like a disheartening self-contradiction: The church, which (as we shall see) lives by the Spirit, often opposes vigorously those groups and persons who most emphasize the Spirit of God in their lives. The church takes this attitude whenever it considers that they have become boastful of the reality of God in their experience and are making extravagant claims as a result.

With these preliminary cautions in mind, we may proceed

to a *working* definition (that is, a signpost): THE HOLY
SPIRIT IS GOD PRESENT AS POWER WITH HIS PEOPLE. All the
words are important enough to be examined in detail. Three
principal ideas require our attention.

To begin, the Holy Spirit is *God present*. The Holy Spirit
is not some sort of impersonal force, such as radiation, which
God sends in his stead, but is God himself.[8] The importance
of this point may be more clearly seen if we consider the question of how the first-century Jesus functions as Savior in the
individual's twentieth-century life. There are, of course, historical relationships: His teachings have been transmitted by
the church which taught them to you and me. The Christianity based on Jesus has affected the life of everyone in our
western civilization whether he is a believer or not. (For example, the social conscience of our society is partly the result
of Christian influence, and even the atheist, in denying God,
usually denies a *Christian* God). But, theologically speaking,
what actually relates Jesus effectively to present-day man is
God himself. The Christian believes that when in his inmost
self he is *confronted by* the summons of Jesus to follow, he
is not simply *thinking about* a first-century Jew whose teachings are still attractive (though this possibility is not excluded); rather, he believes that somehow the recurrent reality
of Jesus meets him and calls for his obedience. Why does this
encounter happen? Theological thinking grapples with this
problem and concludes that God himself has made this reality
of Jesus directly present to each person.[9] Another way to say
this is that the Holy Spirit has related Jesus to the person.

Next, the Holy Spirit is *God present with his people*, col-
lectively, and not simply with persons individually. Here the
phrase "his people" refers to the church. The Spirit of God
is known to persons but not privately. We must clarify this
statement.

There is no doubt that there is something irreducibly personal about the work of the Holy Spirit. No one can draw

a sharp line between the Spirit of God and the spirit of man, even though we know that such a distinction must be made. There is no element in a person's experience that is purely divine; a Geiger counter can locate radioactive elements in the earth, but there is no way to locate divine elements in human experience. Nevertheless, Christians believe that they have met Another. Moreover, this meeting is so intensely personal that it cannot be duplicated by any other person. The experience of Mr. A cannot be repeated by Mr. B because these are two different persons, each with his own life-history. Obviously, this specifically personal element is present in every human experience, whether one is watching a boxing match or hearing a symphony. In the same way, the Spirit is present in a way which is unique for each person. Therefore, it is important for Christians to listen to one another, especially if they do not agree. We can learn about the Spirit's work from one another because each person has something distinctive to contribute. When we begin to hear each other, we often discover that each in his own way has been grasped by the same Spirit (as Paul maintains in 1 Corinthians 12: 4-11).

All of this means that the Spirit is *confessed* only by the church. It does not mean, of course, that the Spirit is *present* only to Christians, for clearly (and fortunately) the work of God is not limited to the church. What it does imply is that the church is the community of persons who confess that they have been met by God. Such a conviction may underlie the fact that Acts never reports anyone's receiving the Spirit privately; rather, the Spirit always comes to persons who are part of the people of God. This is because the Spirit relates the individual not only to God in Christ, but to other believers as well. In this sense, we may say that the Spirit is social.

One of Paul's major problems with the Corinthian church was the failure of those Christians to see this fact (1 Corinthians 12-14). They believed that they had personal experiences of the Spirit which were so powerful, so effective that they no longer needed the rest of the congregation. They came to think that they could dispense with the fellowship of believers because they had met God in the inner sanctum of the soul. Therefore they placed great value on being able to talk about personal religious experience. Having experiences of particular intensity and duration came to be prized because these seemed to guarantee to the individual his own self-sufficient experience of God. Paul, on the other hand, insisted that any religious experience which produced such pride and disruption of the church's life was of no value. Rather, he said, the Spirit of God strengthens the community of believers: "Since you are eager for manifestations of the Spirit, strive to excel in building up the church" (1 Corinthians 14:12).

In speaking of the Spirit and the church, we must avoid two equally destructive extremes. One is the attempt to capture the Spirit for the church, to assume (and even to assert) that the Spirit not only works through the organized church but that he never works against the organization. In fact, however, no church can correctly assume that its voice is always the voice of God's Spirit. At most, it can believe that God's Spirit is present with the spirit of Christian men, and act accordingly. This correction underlies Paul's statement, "When we cry 'Abba! Father!' it is the Spirit himself bearing witness with our spirit that we are children of God" (Romans 8:15-16); that is, the words of the church are never simply and unambiguously the words of God himself. It is essential to be careful about this distinction, not only to avoid blasphemy but in order to recognize that God does, from time to time, set men against the church for its own sake. There may be another Luther!

The other extreme to be avoided grows out of this very possibility, for there is an opposite danger in thinking that one's personal religious experience provides ample warrant for being simply disruptive and anti-ecclesiastical. It is just as important to "test the spirits" when an anti-church, anti-denomination, anti-leadership movement claims to be led by the Spirit of God as it is when ecclesiastical powers assert divine warrant for their own policies. Although the results are opposite (for or against an organized church), the cause is precisely the same — the claim that one's ideas have been given directly by God himself. Whether claimed as divine warrant for promoting the organization's power or as warrant for opposing it (both are often ways of promoting one's own power), this kind of confidence rests really on failure to distinguish between the Spirit of God and the spirit of man. Paul says (in the passage just quoted) that, even in the highest moment of prayer, God's Spirit and man's spirit work in tandem but are not identical. Whenever someone closes this gap between God's Spirit and man's spirit so that he identifies his own convictions with God's, he creates a demon.

The third emphasis in our definition of the Holy Spirit is *God present as power*. This presence is not sheer force, though at times it may include physical strength as in certain Old Testament stories (*e.g.,* Judges 14:5-9; 1 Samuel 11:5-11). It is better to think of this power as the enabling presence of God. Even in the earlier Old Testament writings it was said that the men who built the portable shrine for the Hebrews, the tabernacle and the ark, were enabled to do this work by the Spirit of God (Exodus 35:30-35). Surely this statement does not mean that clumsy workmen were suddenly transformed into skilled craftsmen. Rather, it means that their skills became recognized as gifts of God for the service of God. The same sort of idea lies behind the hope for a leader who would be Spirit-endowed so that he could govern wisely and justly (Isaiah 11). Basically, the Pentecost story makes the same point — that the coming of God's Spirit enabled the apostles to communicate the gospel effectively. This is why Luke does not say that the Spirit simply started some sort of holy bab-

bling of divine words, but rather that apostles began intelligible speech which other men could understand. When
Jesus closed the door to the power politics of Christendom,
he promised a different kind of power which would enable the
disciples to witness. Though they would not have the authority to administer society in the name of Jesus, they would
be enabled to keep their integrity under fire and to bear
effective witness.

The enabling work of the Spirit is not limited to such
special circumstances, of course. Actually, it runs through
the entire Christian life, for, without this, nobody comes to
believe the gospel in the first place or live according to it in
the next. Thus Paul, for example, can say that no one confesses Jesus as Lord without the enabling work of the Spirit
(1 Corinthians 12:1-3); that the Spirit of God enables us to
believe that through Jesus we are real sons and heirs of God
just as Jesus was (Romans 8:14-17); that the Spirit enables
us to pray (Romans 8:26-27); and that the Spirit is the means
by which our mortal bodies will ultimately be transformed
(Romans 8:9-11). In fact, the enabling work of the Spirit
of God as described in Romans 8 stands in clear contrast to
all the things Paul himself could not do as outlined in Romans 7. For Paul, life in the presence of the Spirit was neither
an option nor a mark of a Christian elite, but the irreducible
minimum of Christian existence.

THE SPIRIT IN TODAY'S CHURCH

These remarks about the Spirit are far too sketchy to be
more than guidelines and direction finders. Yet they may
help us get our bearings in a very intricate and important matter and perhaps help us ask some questions about our own
churches.

Frankly, it is not easy to think about the Spirit in the life
of the churches. Besides the embarrassments we noted earlier,
there are three other hurdles.

One hurdle is the fact that the churches we actually know often seem bereft of the Spirit. Whether the ecclesiastical machinery whirs or grinds with "activities" and good works, the church often seems to operate without any conviction that God's presence is what makes it run. Rather, it appears to be the know-how of the pastor, the energy of the boards, the vitality of the community at large, etc., etc. On a state and national level, the life of a denomination is more readily gauged by the efficiency of its bureaucratic structure, the speed of its mailing, the power of its boards and agencies, the size of its investments. We tend to think of the entire operation of the church in precisely the same way as we think of the chambers of commerce or General Motors. The more we use the yardsticks of business, industry, and community agencies to measure the work and power of the church, the less prepared we are to think about the power of the Spirit in its life. To talk about the power of the Spirit in the modern congregation is regarded as naive. If we think of it at all, we are tempted to smile and say with a holy tone, "Of course, God's Spirit is at work in all of this." Perhaps it is — but we cannot escape the feeling that a significant gulf separates our church from Luke's portrait of the fathers in the faith.

We find it hard to talk about the Spirit in the life of the church, secondly, because we are reluctant to speak of our deeds as the work of God. For many persons, this is not only too pious but too proud a thing to say. This reluctance to claim God's power for our own power-plays must be respected, for it is altogether too easy to "take the name of the Lord in vain" by using it as a shield behind which we manipulate committees, badger the opposition, and generally throw our weight around. Everyone has sat on committees in which the opening and closing prayers did not succeed in taking the sting out of actions and attitudes which were distinctly out of keeping with the spirit of Christian brothers facing policy decisions. Instinctively, we are made cynical when we hear later that such decisions are labeled as "great things God is doing in our midst."

A third reason we avoid talking about the Spirit in the church is that common sense tells us that not everything promoted in the name of the Spirit is in fact the work of the Spirit. Not only Martin Luther but Elmer Gantry has claimed the support of God. This problem is not new, of course; nor is it avoidable. But in our time, most people are unwilling to criticize a religious idea or program. We are too tolerant of everything done in the name of religion or faith to be willing to "test the spirits" — that is, to risk saying that this or that act cannot claim God's Spirit as its true source of power.

These hurdles are formidable, but they are not insurmountable. Luke's own story has some suggestions built in; we call attention to several.

1. We note first that the disciples had to *wait* for the *promised* Spirit. Nothing they could do would force him to come quickly or at their convenience. This starting-point is important, because it reminds us that there exists no set of directions for generating the presence of the Holy Spirit. In this light, exhortations to "be more spiritual" are beside the point. So are all attempts to induce God's Spirit to empower us, whether one dims the lights to create reverence during the pastoral prayer or has the organist "play something soft" (!) during communion. No manipulation of the congregation's emotions can possibly induce the Spirit to make himself known; the Spirit is free, and this includes freedom from human control of every kind. At the same time, this inability to elicit the Spirit must not make us indifferent to the possible presence of God. Plowing does not make it rain, but does make it possible for things to grow if it rains. Likewise, there are things we can do which are appropriate to the work of the Spirit; at the same time, doing them, and doing them well, is no guarantee that God will meet us as we go about our work.

The clear need to depend on God's decision to be present to us is one side of the matter; the other side is the fact that the Christian is confident that he does not wait in vain, for the Jesus in whom he believes has promised the Spirit's presence. Moreover, a basic element of Christian faith and life is the inner assurance that God is always present, whether a person knows it or not, for we are reminded of the danger of "quenching the Spirit."

Both emphases must be made: the sense of depending on God alone for his presence, and the sense of assurance that God is present despite one's failure to be aware of it. The former must be said lest we think God is always present by default (as if he had not willed to be with us) ; the latter must be said lest we suggest that the Christian gambles with the chances that God might or might not be present at a specific time.

What do these considerations imply for our situation? Perhaps the most important single thing is an attitude of expectancy that God will really be present with his people. Far too few services of worship, for example, are marked by this attitude. They are more like memorial services to the memory of the times when God was present. Nurturing the sense of expectancy that God will be present as we sing and pray, preach and give, means cultivating a trust in God's promise, a trust which is so simple that it is hard to achieve because it is easier to think of God than to trust him.

2. Expecting God's presence leads us to think about God's *will.* If it is really God whom we expect, then we are expecting to be met by a Thou with a will to make known, a summons to deliver. In other words, we cannot expect God without expecting that we must act. Believing in the Holy Spirit saves us from simply holding theological ideas; rather, it puts us on the line to decide whether we will act in accordance with our belief or not.

In this connection, Luke shows that when God's presence

communicated power, the disciples were galvanized into action. They found themselves evolving a new kind of life. We will deal with this in Chapter 4. Here, we simply point out that emphasizing the personal presence of God is by no means an invitation to retreat from the complexities of life into a serene inwardness "away from it all."

We can go quickly to the heart of the matter: A fundamental task of the church is to make actual an alternative to the kind of life people normally live, not simply to talk about what it would be like if everyone did as Jesus did. But, frankly, life in church and among Christian people is virtually indistinguishable from that found in a lodge, union, or club. The church today simply does not present an alternative to society, but is simply society on Sunday. The fact that pulpits present all manner of exhortation and advice does not affect this statement whatsoever, for, as Paul once observed, "The Kingdom of God does not consist in talk but in power" (1 Corinthians 4:20). Yet, unless the church offers a different caliber of life from that available elsewhere, there is no adequate reason for the church to exist. Simply having another theory about man and the world is not sufficient justification, unless it produces — at least here and there — a new kind of life, a genuine alternative. Today's churches, which are as nervous about their popularity ratings as TV shows, have slipped back into that twilight zone between Easter and Pentecost when the church believed in Jesus' resurrection but was powerless to act. Then, as now, the disciples sat around and talked about the resurrection without demonstrating it.

How can congregations begin? Launching an alternative does not depend on an auspicious program engineered by committee planners (though this too is a form of stewardship not to be despised by people who think they are "spiritual"). If the Spirit is the enabling presence of God, then the place to begin is with whatever genuine convictions the congregation may have. Trusting the Spirit of God means being willing to act on those convictions with the confidence that God's presence will make possible an act of witness with integrity. The question of whether that act brings "success" is an entirely different matter which may not have anything whatever to do with the power of the Spirit. After all, the devil succeeds too!

When the church trusts God's presence as power in order to risk actualizing the life it talks about, then it will not retreat from the problems of society, from issues such as war and peace, racism and equality. Acts shows that the voice of the church in such matters will then not be simply the expression of its opinions, even correct ones. Rather, its voice will be expressed through the quality of its life, as influenced by the presence of God. With such a witness, the church can then speak in conviction and power. I suspect that then it will also be heard. The church today does not need new analyses of its plight but a readiness to put into gear those insights it already possesses. Trusting the Holy Spirit does not mean idle waiting for a soul-shattering event that will dissolve the problems of society painlessly but a willingness to act now, trusting God to be present as power when we do. As we shall see, Acts can be regarded as the story of the early church's experience of being nudged into doing God's will through the enabling presence of God's Spirit.

3. Implicit in Acts but explicit in Paul is a third suggestion: The results of the Spirit's presence are *ethical*. This relationship is clear in Paul's list of the "fruits of the Spirit" in Galatians 5 and in his discussion of the work of the Spirit in 1 Corinthians 12-14. This is an important insight for the matter of "testing the spirits." It is valuable for more than merely determining whether other people's claims about the Spirit are valid, though it includes this possibility. Perhaps more consistently important is the testing of ourselves. To put it directly, ethical conduct offers real evidence that God is present and empowers the believer to live as he does. (Evidence is not proof, of course!)

The decisive evidence of God's presence, therefore, is not some unusual experience, such as excited speech or gifts of "faith healing" as the Corinthians thought (and some people think now), though these obviously do occur. Rather, the decisive evidence is ethical, or as Paul puts it, the consequence of the Spirit is love. By this statement he did not mean simply a warm-hearted romanticism (which always prefers to say that the fruit of love is the Spirit!). What Paul had in mind is a rather sober, yet amazingly possible, consistent concern for another person as is sketched in 1 Corinthians 13.

We may further say that, rather than asking whether a person has a throbbing religious experience or holds an avant-garde idea, a better test of whether the Spirit is present is whether he finds it possible, at least one day at a time, to love another person without exploiting him. Here is why the First Epistle of John, which says, "By this you know the Spirit of God: every spirit which confesses that Jesus has come in the flesh is of God" (4:2), puts equal emphasis on love of one's brother (2:7-11; 3:11-24). A word of caution is needed. "Testing the spirits" is not making a checklist on fellow Christians to see whether they live up to our codes of conduct. Rather it is looking for tokens of God's presence in those dimensions of life which make concrete what God enables men to be and do; specifically, this means that we test the spirits by asking whether we can live in the world as Jesus himself did (1 John 2:1-6).

We are often distressed by the inability of the church to deal with concrete problems of race, peace, narcotics, sex, alcoholism, and civic corruption. Yet this also reveals, in an impoverished way, the integrity of the church, for lofty pronouncements made by committees must ring hollow and stand as empty gestures so long as the congregations themselves are not dealing with these matters day by day. This "thin" congregational life has nothing really authentic to say. Therefore, denominational convention resolutions have almost no impact, even on the churches which circulate them. In matters of racial tension or sex standards, many congregations simply have nothing to offer that is not already being provided by *Ladies Home Journal* and *Life*. The reason is that the churches have regarded the fruit of the Spirit merely as the ability to be "religious." However, the fruits of the Spirit, as Paul catalogues them, point in another direction, and suggest that the work of the Spirit is not to make it possible for a man to be "spiritual" but to be genuinely "secular" — that is, to enable him to bring his day-to-day life into the orbit of his commitment to God in Christ. The voice of the church will have new timbre when it does more than simply pronounce, and begins to actualize what its constituents confess in faith. When this change occurs, the church's words in social matters will be witness-words grounded in a style of life it has forged by the presence of God himself. Until then, it may not make any difference what the church pronounces. When the congregation risks acting on its affirmations, it will discover that God's Spirit is with them.

CHAPTER THREE

HOW IS JESUS GOOD NEWS?

Let it be known to you therefore, brethren, that through this man [Jesus] forgiveness of sins is proclaimed to you. . . .
—St. Paul (Acts 13:38)

In the Christian view, Adam's fall simultaneously precipitated the corruption of the whole world. The solidarity of mankind, on this account, is a corollary of its common sinfulness. . . . By contrast, the post-Christian ethic establishes solidarity on the basis of man's innocence of the absurdity of the world. The great difference lies in this: the Christian ethic is an ethic of forgiveness; the post-Christian ethic is an ethic of innocence.*
—Gabriel Vahanian

TEXT OF ACTS: 2:14-42; 10:30-48; 13:13-43

THINGS TO LOOK FOR:

1. In Acts 2:14-36, note the themes of the sermon: that the coming of the Spirit is what the Bible talked about long ago in Joel's writing (Joel 2:28-32); and that Jesus is the "Lord" through whom men may be saved, for the words of the Psalms apply only to him and not to David (their traditional author). Notice also what is and is not said about Jesus. How does this differ from the presentation of Jesus in sermons preached today? How would you react to this kind of sermon next Sunday? Why?

2. Acts 10:30-48 is part of a story that stretches from 10:1 to 11:18. Notice what is said about Jesus in this sermon (10:34-43). Observe how important the idea of witness is. See this theme also in 1:8, 22; 2:32; 3:15; 5:32; 13:31; 22:15, 20; 26:16. What does the word "witness" really mean for Luke? Note that the same Greek word is translated "martyr."

3. The sermon in Acts 13:16-41 is part of a larger story, 13:13-52. The whole scene is part of the so-called first missionary journey of Paul, which begins at 13:1. Paul here is in central Asia Minor, and is invited to preach in the synagogue according to the custom. Those who "fear God" are probably Gentiles who attend the synagogue but refuse to become full Jews through circumcision and accepting the Jewish way of life. The sermon falls into three parts: (a) Jesus is the Son of David (this phrase is a symbolic way of saying he is the Messiah, for according to Jewish hope the Messiah would be a descendant of David); (b) because Jesus was raised from the dead, God fulfills his promise to Israel through him; (c) therefore forgiveness of sins is available through Jesus.

4. Note that similar themes run through these sermons. How is the story of Jesus good news for these hearers?

5. Jesus told a two-pronged parable about forgiveness (Matthew 18:23-35). Read this carefully to discover what you can about the nature and result of forgiveness. Try putting the parable into modern terms.

HOW IS JESUS GOOD NEWS?

IN A WORLD WITHOUT CHRISTENDOM IT IS NO LONGER OBVIOUS TO all that the gospel is trustworthy or true. Today, anyone who commends the gospel to another has a difficult task. Whether he be a preacher in the pulpit or a commuter in a bus, he must be prepared to show why anybody ought to believe it enough to put his life into the hands of Jesus — an ancient Jew who was abandoned by friends and executed with criminals because the accredited spokesmen for God judged him to be a fraud. Anyone who wants to win friends to such a faith today must be prepared to show its rationale. That is, he must be some kind of theologian. The mere Bible-quoter is believable only to those who have never deeply doubted the gospel in the first place; he has nothing to say to persons who are cut off from the Christian tradition. To tell them that "the Bible says. . . ." is not enough, for they simply shrug their shoulders, "So what?" This basic absence of belief in Christian assumptions runs through our culture, and results from the death of Christendom.

This is not simply a picture of the unchurched. Despite full pews, many persons within the churches are in precisely the same situation. The fact that churches are full does not mean that people are really hearing the gospel or believing it; it may simply mean that Christendom is not yet quite dead everywhere, and that the church-habit is hard to break in a society which places a premium on conforming. Many people within the church think that Christianity is a system of basic religious truths, eternal verities, and principles of action — religion in general and morals in excellence. They see no reason, however, why the story of Jesus should be considered good news.

In other words, our situation is marked by two things: One is that many persons in the church do not know what we are talking about when we present the gospel as outlined in the New Testament; the other is that there is a growing number of people who couldn't care less whether we said anything about Jesus at all. The point of the gospel has become dulled for those within the church, and the gospel meaning of Jesus has competition outside the church. Both factors force us to see that believing in Jesus is a deliberate act of faith. In a world without Christendom, men no longer become believers by default. We need to sharpen this need for faith-commitment by contrasting it with various ways of viewing Jesus.

Ways of Understanding Jesus

We begin by noting three ways of looking at Jesus which differ from that in Acts. Then we examine Acts.

1. Jesus is often seen as a tragedy. His life story, in this view, is that of a good man who failed. It is the account of the inevitable destruction of a good man by the evil forces around him. Jesus is a heroic martyr-figure towering above the heads of his contemporaries, but in the last analysis he is considered a failure because he did not get his people to understand. His followers misunderstood him too, and transformed him into a divine savior. For example, Robert Graves and Joshua Podro write:

> A close scrutiny of the Gospels reveals the astonishing paradox that Jesus, an apocalyptic Pharisee whose message was neither unorthodox nor original, came by a series of accidents and misunderstandings to be posthumously worshipped as a

heathen God—to use "heathen" in its strict Old Testament
sense [Gentile]—and was only then rejected by his own nation.[1]

Those who insist that the church perverted the pure teaching
of Jesus usually blame Paul. Thus Graves and Podro comment that, after Paul had established himself as the leader of
obstreperous Christians, "the falsifying of Jesus' own doctrine
by the publication of tendentious Greek Gospels now began"
(page 821). Even so, his tragic figure looms over the heads of
his misunderstanding followers. This portrait of Jesus is more
common than we may think. If there is any good news here
at all, it consists of the possibility of throwing away Christianity in order to salvage the true Jesus and to appropriate his
pure religion — if possible.

2. Jesus is sometimes presented as the greatest of the prophets, the good teacher, the clearest interpreter of God's love.
Liberal Christianity, especially, has championed this view.
One does not need to impugn Jesus as a teacher to be dis-
satisfied with this interpretation, for it amounts to saying that
in Jesus we have no more than a new edition of what we have
already had in the Old Testament. This is not really good
news but merely a Sunday supplement.

3. Jesus has also been viewed as a religious fool or as a dis-
torter of the truth and a perverter of mankind. We think of
Nietzsche's point that Jesus advocated a slave morality. Not
the meek, but the mighty, shall inherit the earth, said
Nietzsche. Interestingly, Nietzsche has many followers today
who have never heard of him. Even within the churches,
there are people who do not really believe Jesus was right.
They piously praise the Sermon on the Mount while actually
believing it to be irrelevant.

This list of alternatives is far from complete, but it is long
enough to suggest that today the story of Jesus is not inevitably good news, because there are other ways of looking
at him. Anyone who wants to commend this story as news

that is good for modern man must be prepared to explain it and defend it. To do so, he must understand it — at least understand something about its essential elements.

We are not the first generation of believers to have had this problem on our hands. In fact, the decay of Christendom has put us all on the frontiers of faith, and it is here that we find the New Testament. This literature was born on the frontier. This is one reason why the Book of Acts can be of help. It shows how other frontiersmen presented the story of Jesus as good news in a world without Christendom.

The easiest place to see this frontier spirit is in the sermons in Acts.[2] We begin with the sermon outline Peter used when he presented the story of Jesus to the Roman army officer, Cornelius. The whole story runs from 10:1 to 11:18. The narrative part will be studied in the next chapter; here we concentrate on the sermon outline found in 10:34-43.

We begin by noting that, in the sermon, verses 34 and 35 form an introduction; they contain a remark which is appropriate for the occasion. All the speeches in Acts begin in a similar way. Verse 36 is a kind of title for the outline that follows. The actual outline begins in verse 37 and has three sentences in the Greek text. Each makes a point: (1) God was at work in Jesus' life; (2) God raised him from the dead and made us witnesses; (3) the Old Testament points ahead to the good news that in Jesus' name there is forgiveness of sins. We shall analyze each point in some detail. This procedure will open up the logic of one way of looking at Jesus as good news.

1. God was at work in the mission of Jesus. Only three things are accented: his baptism, his deeds of healing, and his death. This is about as short an outline of Jesus' life as the New Testament contains. The death of Jesus is described in phrases which echo the Old Testament, and the word "crucify" does not occur at all. The "anointing" of Jesus refers to his baptism and is a kind of pun on the word "Christ" or "Messiah." We might catch the pun by translating the phrase

as "God messiahed him." Notice that there is no hint of Jesus' birth or his teachings. These omissions offend modernist and fundamentalist alike; nevertheless, the old outline did not regard these items as being essential to the good news about Jesus.

But why can this be called an outline of good news anyway? One thing is clear. The news is not good simply because Jesus "went about doing good" or because he cast out demons or even because God was "with him." Each of these statements may be perfectly true without being in any way good news. They might simply tell about a devout man's good life. This point is important because it reminds us that the gospel is not simply the story of a good man named Jesus who did great things in the name of God. This information may be true, and it may be interesting, but it is not in itself news that is good.[8]

2. The second point is more important: "God raised him [from the dead ones] . . . and made him manifest" (10:40). Here is the decisive point. Without this, Jesus may be viewed as a man whose career is interesting and even important, but actually no more decisive for me than the life of Socrates or Jeremiah. But his resurrection implies that Jesus is not simply an exceptionally good Jew; he is the absolutely decisive man for every man. We shall come back to this matter.

Verse 41 makes an important qualification. God made the resurrected Jesus visible only to the disciples. This limitation is in clear contrast to the broad knowledge of his public career, emphasized by the introductory words "You know" (10:36). This distinction is a decisive detail. The mission of Jesus is public knowledge. It can be investigated by anyone who has the interest and the training to do so, whether he be Christian, Moslem, Jew, or agnostic. But the resurrection is different. The historian can study what the disciples thought about it and he can analyze the stories they told about it, but he cannot deal with the resurrection itself. The resurrection is accessible only to the man to whom the Risen One has been made manifest. We have no tools to study resurrections; we can study only stories of resurrections. If it happened, the resurrection of Jesus is unique. It must not be confused with stories about men coming back to life again like Lazarus, because resurrection means transformation, and not simply resuscitation. The resurrection did not simply restore Jesus to life; it transformed him completely.

Now, frankly, some people are embarrassed by the fact that the resurrection is not a public event, for this means there is no neutral evidence that Jesus was raised and transformed. There are only the reports of the Christians who say they have met the Resurrected One.

At first, this lack of evidence is strange in light of the fact that Acts reports that the disciples claimed to be witnesses of the resurrection (see, for example, Acts 3:14f; 5:30-32). But as we read the Gospel According to Luke, we find that not a single disciple was on the scene when it happened. In fact, no one in the entire New Testament record saw Jesus in the process of being resurrected. How can anyone be a witness to the resurrection if he did not see it happen?

Our sermon outline gives the answer. The true witness to the resurrection is not some bystander who saw Jesus come out of the tomb but the person who has been apprehended by the Risen One. Thus the witness to the resurrection of Jesus is at the same time a witness to his own experience. He does not witness to what he saw but to Whom he met; he is not a witness *of* the resurrection event but a witness *to* it. This experience was the only real evidence the first believers had, but it was enough. Matthew knows that empty tombs prove nothing at all except that they are empty, and recognizes that, so far as this kind of evidence goes, a thief could have emptied it also (Matthew 28:11-15). The fact is that no Christian can demonstrate *historically* that Jesus was resurrected. Every Christian believer can, however, testify (bear witness) to the resurrection because he has met the Living One and been transformed by him. For this reason, Luke emphasizes that the disciples went into the world as witnesses to the resurrection.

Not long after Luke wrote, someone attempted to get around this embarrassing situation by reporting the resurrection differently. This report is found in the so-called Gospel of Peter, which is not part of our Bible. We quote the crucial passage in Chapter 8:

> And the Elders were afraid and came unto Pilate, entreating him and saying: Give us soldiers that we may watch his sepulchre for three days, lest his disciples come and steal him away. . . . And Pilate gave them Petronius the centurion with soldiers to watch the sepulchre; and the elders and scribes came with them unto the tomb, and when they had rolled a great stone to keep out the centurion and the soldiers, then all that were there together set it upon the door of the tomb; and plastered thereon seven seals; and they pitched a tent there and kept watch. . . . Now in the night whereon the Lord's day dawned, as the soldiers were keeping guard two by two in every watch, there came a great sound in the heaven and *they saw* the heavens opened and two men descend thence. . . . And that stone . . . rolled away of itself and went back to the side, and the sepulchre was opened and both of the young men entered in. When therefore those *soldiers saw* that, they waked up the centurion and the elders (for they also were there keeping watch); and while they were yet telling them the things which they had seen, *they saw* again three men come out of the sepulchre. . . . And *they heard* a voice out of the heavens saying, Hast thou preached unto them that sleep? And an answer was heard from the cross, saying Yea.⁴

Here the dilemma of the embarrassed Christian is resolved: The facts of the resurrection no longer depend only on the reports of supposedly biased Christians, but on neutral eyewitnesses. In this account, people saw the resurrection who did not become believers. This gospel became quite popular at first, and we can see why. But the church did not regard it as trustworthy, and refused to let it into the New Testament.

The irony is that today many Christians who have never heard of the Gospel of Peter still represent its point of view, and speak of Jesus' resurrection as if it were the same kind of public event as Glenn's orbiting the earth. The irony is further compounded by the fact that those who treat the resurrection of Jesus in this way often want to be known as orthodox Christians, although this gospel was rejected long ago because it flirted with heresy. The writer of Acts is wiser. He admits that the resurrection of Jesus is knowable only to those who have become witnesses to it by meeting the Lord. No historical study proves that the Christian gospel is right; rather, all historical study pushes us to the frontier where the question must be decided on faith.

This second point of the sermon outline does not come into focus for us until we see verse 42. The resurrected Jesus is announced to be the Judge-designate. The outline puts it this way: "He is the one ordained by God to be the judge of the living and the dead." Without this point, we might be tempted to think of the resurrection as something tremendous that happened to *him* but which has no relation to us at all. Without this statement that the resurrected Lord is the Judge-designate, we might believe the story of Easter and comment, "Terrific! But after all, that was Jesus. What has that got to do with us?" Verse 42 answers this question by linking our destiny to that of Jesus, for it tells us that Jesus is every man's Judge. This statement says that the man whom God designated to judge us is the man executed on Golgotha and raised on Easter. If, then, our destiny depends on the verdict of this Judge, we must recognize that the story of Jesus is the story of the one who will be the arbiter of our status before God. Suddenly for each individual, the story of Jesus is transformed from a piece of interesting ancient history to the disclosure of "where my destiny hangs." This change makes the story of Jesus real news. But it still does not show why this is *good* news; it could just as well be bad news. To see why this announcement about Jesus is good news, we need the third point of the old sermon outline.

3. Here it is: "To him [that is, to Jesus] all the prophets bear witness that every one who believes in him receives forgiveness of sins through his name." These words transform the information about Jesus into the good news for all mankind. According to this early sketch of the gospel, the good news consists of the headline that the Judge forgives those who believe on his name. That is, he forgives those who believe he is really the Judge. Here is the heart of the good news in this sermon: The Judge forgives.

The sermons reported in Acts 2 and 13 may now be quickly compared with this one. They too put the gospel in terms of forgiveness.

There are other word pictures for the good news, and each of them highlights an aspect of the good news not emphasized by the others. The New Testament uses words like "reconciliation," "redemption," "regeneration," "rebirth" (notice the emphasis on "re-" — that is, doing again!), etc. Each "salvation-word" can be studied profitably; but, since Acts deals with forgiveness, this is the word we shall explore.

THE LOGIC OF FORGIVENESS

Before examining the logic of forgiveness, we must remind ourselves that all language about salvation comes in clusters of ideas. Each word-picture has its own peculiar emphasis to make. Each word for salvation brings three ideas with it: a picture of the human situation, the remedy necessary, and the meaning of Jesus as the bringer of the remedy. For example, the word "reconciliation" describes the work of Jesus in healing estrangement. Thus one cannot talk about reconciliation without implying that man is estranged from God and from himself, and that Jesus as savior is the reconciler of God and man. In the same way, talking about rebirth requires us to say things about a once-born person, then to show how the rebirth of a person takes place and specifically how it takes place through Jesus. Each word-picture must be allowed to make its own point with its own cluster of ideas, so that it can guide us to an aspect of the gospel not seen through other words. Thinking about the meaning of Jesus requires that we think with the grain of the words we use. Otherwise, every-thing is confused.

When we turn to the idea of forgiveness, we find that we are faced with three issues: What is it that must be forgiven? What happens in forgiveness? What does this have to do with Jesus? Exploring the good news as forgiveness requires us to examine each of these.

The news of forgiveness tells us that sin is a debt. The form of the Lord's Prayer used in Matthew illustrates this concept perfectly: "Forgive us our debts." Another version, "forgive us our trespasses," interprets the idea of "debt" but dulls the point to do it. Talking about forgiveness assumes a situation of indebtedness.

Forgiveness is not simply another word for reconciliation, even though the two terms are often used interchangeably. To speak about forgiveness is possible only if there is a debt to be forgiven, an obligation to be canceled. Debts cannot be recon-ciled; one might reconcile the amount of the indebtedness, but the debt itself must be either paid or forgiven. Reconciliation implies estrangement; this cannot be canceled, for it can only be resolved by the restoration of good relations. We may ap-pear to be splitting hairs, but actually we are attempting to think straight about the words we use when we speak of Jesus as the good news.

Most people do not like to think of their relationship to God in commercial terms, in terms of debts. But why should we avoid such terms? The New Testament writers were not finicky about where they found words to talk about man and God and Jesus: The law court gave them "justification," the slave market contributed "redemption," the temple gave them "sacrifice," the farm gave "vine and branches," the sheep pen gave "the good shepherd," and the gymnasium gave "the race" and "the runner."

As far as "debt" and "forgiveness" are concerned, it is important to remember not only the words of the Lord's Prayer but also Jesus' parable about the debtor (Matthew 18:23-35). This parable makes precisely the same point as we have been outlining. It should be read carefully; we will come back to it.

Our real difficulty with talking about sin as debt is that this concept treats sin as if it were an objective thing, measurable and payable. Yet, even within this difficulty we find a value. In our day we tend to subjectify everything. Therefore, for the sake of balance, we need words that point to both the objective and the subjective meanings of sin. The value of talking about salvation in terms of reconciliation between persons is that it points us to the personal, subjective resolution of our relation to God and man; the virtue of talking about debts and forgiveness is to remind us that sin is more than personal estrangement — it is also an objective fact. Let me use a brutal example. The planned extermination of the Jews of Europe by Hitler's henchmen was not simply a matter of personal estrangement from God; it was also a horrendous, objective fact. This sin is not simply what happened to the Nazis (subjective) but is also what happened to the Jews (objective). Talking about forgiveness reminds us that sin is no mere kink in the soul; it is also the actual doing of deeds which violate the will of God and the nature of man. Talking about forgiveness drives us to see that man is a debtor, that he stands under the objective fact of his sins.

How does man get into this situation? How does he get to be a debtor? To begin with, he is born with a mortgage in his hands. That is, he is born with the obligation to obey God. Wherever man does the will of God, he is meeting this obligation. But he defaults on the obligation again and again. He defaults when he pretends he does not have to obey, when

1. Born w/ obligation. (debt)

he makes himself God, when he simply ignores God's will. Thus, not only is he born into a situation in which he is under obligation to pay, but he finds himself behind in payments, and soon the debts pyramid. Every man is born into a situation in which he is under obligation to God; he is also born into a family of man with a fantastic pile of back-payments, and to this accumulation he adds his own failures to obey. This is not a pleasant picture, but it is one we understand.

If man is the debtor, God is the creditor. He is the one to whom the debt is owed. This relationship means that judgment must be pictured as the settling of the accounts, the foreclosing of the mortgage, the response which must be made on the day the note falls due — precisely as in Jesus' parable! At the same time, forgiveness means that God will refuse to collect from us what we owe, that he will not force us into bankruptcy even though we cannot pay. Forgiveness means that God marks our obligation "paid in full," just as Jesus said in the parable.

Another example may shed more light. The forgiven man may be regarded as the pardoned criminal who leaves the prison a free man. His crime stands as an objective fact; nothing will restore the lives of those he has murdered. But his pardon by the governor means that, from this day forward, society will no longer deal with him on the basis of those crimes. He is free to start over. He is not released from the obligation of obeying the law; he is released from being treated as a lawbreaker. This is why one New Testament interpreter has talked about forgiveness as a situation of freedom, freedom from the past and freedom for the future.[5]

Now such a way of dealing with objective sin and guilt is clearly immoral. It violates an important principle of morality — that of fair recompense. But this is just the point: Forgiveness cannot be earned. Forgiveness ruptures ethics because it plants a question mark behind the whole system of rewards for good and bad deeds. This is precisely what the Bible talks about when it says there is good news in the story of Jesus, for the gospel is addressed to criminals waiting for their trial. It tells us that we are forgiven even before our trial comes up on Judgment Day.

What, then, has this to do with Jesus? Many things may be said, but only five must be:

1. Forgiveness is not an original Christian idea. The early church inherited from Judaism the belief that God was merciful and that he forgave sinners. The Old Testament affirms this idea again and again. This is why the sermon outline said "The prophets bear witness" to the forgiveness through Jesus. Besides, every year the Day of Atonement offered every Jew a share in divine forgiveness. Moreover, John the Baptist and groups such as the Essenes (who wrote the Dead Sea Scrolls) also preached forgiveness and prepared men to receive it. Therefore, in the streets of Jerusalem around A.D. 35 the Christian offer of forgiveness was not news at all, nor was it a Christian "specialty of the house." The early Christians did not come upon the scene announcing that they had good news that God forgives sinners. What *was* news, however, was the announcement that one could have forgiveness here and now by believing in Jesus — not simply daily forgiveness, but the decisive forgiveness of Judgment Day. This was news, but it was controversial news.

2. God did not invent forgiveness on Good Friday. The death of Jesus did not make it possible for God to do something he could not do before, nor did the death of Jesus bring about a change in God's attitudes or tactics. Rather, the forgiving work of God reached its climax, its fulfillment, in the forgiveness preached through Jesus. Paul saw this new development clearly when he wrote the Romans that what God did in Christ was done "because in his divine forbearance he had passed over former sins" (Rom. 3:25). He was saying that in Jesus God ratified for all time what he had been doing

many times before. Paul's words also imply that, when we speak of Jesus as fulfilling the Old Testament, we mean much more than merely connecting Old Testament verses with Gospel stories. It means that the forgiveness we have through Jesus fulfills the forgiveness the Jews have had long ago and continue to have to this very day. In fact, for us Gentiles, faith in Jesus is the way we come to share the faith of Israel, and the experience of being forgiven by the God of Abraham, Isaac, and Jacob.

3. Jesus preached forgiveness on earth. Not only did he talk about it in the parable we noted, but he actualized this forgiveness in this work. Especially important is Mark 2:1-12. This story reports that Jesus told the lame man, "My son, your sins are forgiven." We must remember that this passive form "are forgiven" is a Palestinian way of saying "God forgave you." Jesus did not say "I forgive you," but announced that God has already done so. What offended the scribes was that Jesus spoke for God, that he dared to say what God had done. The report of the healing that followed was intended to demonstrate that Jesus had been right. Thus we see that what is new with Jesus is not the idea that God forgives but the announcement that God has already done so. Besides, Jesus did not say, "If you repent, God will forgive you and you might even be healed." He simply announced what God had done, and the man was healed when he believed this good news enough to try to walk.

Moreover, Jesus did not lecture people on forgiveness any more than he talked about sin. Instead, he went to sinners and proceeded to show that God had already acted to wipe away the burden of the past. This forgiveness is what he intended his healing work to show (see especially Luke 11:14-23). Since God has already forgiven man, no barrier between persons has any meaning; therefore Jesus went to every kind of person who would receive him, whether Pharisee or prostitute. By eating with sinners and saints alike, Jesus practiced a kind of "open membership" to show that the forgiveness of God was a present reality. This is why Jesus could characterize John's mission as playing funeral, and his own as playing wedding (Luke 7:31-35). Jesus regarded his own work as good news.

4. We must face the question: Was Jesus right or not? Was God's forgiveness already available to men who saw the kingdom in his work, or was it something that might happen if they achieved a particular level of repentance first? On Good Friday afternoon, it seemed pretty certain that Jesus was wrong, that he had been a fraud. After all, the interpreters of God's will had repudiated him and God himself hadn't helped him to escape. And, by fleeing, the disciples were in effect agreeing that Jesus had not been a valid, bona fide spokesman for God.

But the resurrection changed all that. The resurrection ratified Jesus, put a divine seal of approval on his life and work, and on his message of forgiveness as well. The church could preach forgiveness because it remembered that through him God's forgiveness was made actual here and now in history whenever and wherever men would believe Jesus. If God had not raised Jesus, then forgiveness would still be something men must work for, pray for, repent for, hope for on Judgment Day. If God had not raised Jesus, then forgiveness would still be God's gracious response to the repentance of man. But the resurrection ratified the message of this man Jesus who came to announce that God had already forgiven men, that God had already acted, that God had seized the initiative.

Therefore, the resurrection brings a revolution in the theology of forgiveness: Repentance does not bring forgiveness, but forgiveness brings repentance.[6] For Jesus and the early church, repentance was not sorrow for sin, and certainly not regret for getting caught. Rather it was a turning of the whole life of man toward God; especially important, this turning was not done in the hope that God might respond but was itself a response to the news that God had acted first. The lingering effect of Catholicism's system of penance confuses us into thinking that repentance is a preliminary requirement for absolution. The gospel, however, being more Hebraic than Catholic, interprets repentance not as regret but as turning around; its main accent is positive, not negative. Thus the whole life of man is one of repentance, not a life of regret but of joyous turning to the Forgiver. What separates the Protestant from the Hebrew is the conviction that God has already acted prior to man's repentance.

5. The disciples proclaimed forgiveness in Jesus as part of their witness. They knew God forgave them because they met the Risen One, who forgave them and commissioned them. Here is why the story of Peter's denial is so important (Luke 22:31-34, 54-62). We do not have a story of Jesus' meeting Peter alone, but Paul says the risen Lord appeared (first) to Cephas (1 Corinthians 15:3-5); that is, to Peter. From the course of Peter's life, we know that the Lord forgave him, just as he forgave all the others who had fled into the night. In other words, the experience of the resurrection — that is, of meeting the resurrected and ratified one — confirmed to the believers that God had forgiven them. Witnessing to the resurrection, therefore, meant also witnessing to their being forgiven.

SUCH A GOSPEL TODAY?

We must recognize that putting the gospel into such terms brings real problems. There are at least three objections to any gospel of forgiveness.

The first is that people are not at all ready to believe that God forgives anybody. They are prepared to believe in a God of moral law but not in a God who forgives. They are willing to believe that God is a Universal Underwriter who stands behind the moral law and sees to it that every man gets what he deserves, that crime does not pay, that right always triumphs, that right does have might, that there is always a happy ending for the good people of the earth. People can believe in this God because they can figure out where they stand in relation to him, as a student figures his grade-point average on the basis of his papers which have already been returned by the professor. But a God who will not reward or punish on the basis of what men deserve does not appear to be worth worshiping, and even seems to be plainly immoral as well. We really find it unfair for God to send his sunshine on the just and unjust alike, because we think the sinner ought to have either a drought or a flood. In the story of the prodigal son and the forgiving father, we sympathize with the older brother who stayed home to do the work while the kid brother was away living it up. We agree with the older boy who complained when the father threw a party for the wastrel when he returned, and we join him in his protest, "Dad, you're not fair." In exactly the same way, people are prepared to believe in a God who is fair but not in a God who forgives.

A second objection can be put this way: God forgives, but why get excited about it? It is his business to forgive. That is, God has no real choice but to forgive; this is what he is for. Announcing forgiveness, according to this line of reasoning, is not broadcasting good news, but simply recognizing the way things are, and has nothing to do with Jesus.

A third objection to saying that forgiveness is the good news is that this affirmation requires us to accept certain ideas about ourselves and God. Few men will insist that they are blameless, but still fewer will admit that they are personally responsible for their sins and must be forgiven by God. After all, everybody makes mistakes, but are these really anybody's fault? We are all the victims of circumstances, it is said. Our parents spoiled us in the first place, the public schools failed to discipline us in the next; moreover, our society urges us to do whatever we can get by with. Most of all, none of us asked to be born into this kind of world, and, besides, we arrived fairly innocent. In our post-Protestant world, so the argument continues, every artist, musician, and playwright is attempting to show the disintegration of human life and the effects of sin and guilt, but few people feel any personal responsibility for it, and certainly not enough to need forgiveness.

The foregoing is an abbreviated list of objections, but it is enough to cause us to think twice before talking glibly about forgiveness; for that matter, before we believe in it too quickly ourselves.

Still, thinking of the gospel in terms of debt and forgiveness is one of the more promising ways of presenting the good news. For one thing, our commercialized civilization understands business categories better than any other. Saying that God forgives men stretches our imagination, because we can scarcely conceive of a loan company canceling a debt when the borrower cannot pay. Yet, just for this reason, forgiveness is a good category to use; it keeps grace in the gospel. It points to an act of God which has no basis other than the inherent character of God. It reminds us that the gospel is an announcement of the good news of what God has done freely, and not an ad stating that a good arrangement with God is now possible.

Perhaps more important is the fact that forgiveness is something generally lacking in the non-biblical religions which we face. Islam, Buddhism, Hinduism, and Confucianism emphasize religion as moral demand, whether it be a demand for submission or for serenity. For the man who fails, each religion outlines a clear consequence, just as it does for the man who succeeds. The fundamental appeal of Buddhism to western man is that it is a religion without God, salvation without grace, achievement of serenity without the church. But there is no real place in this faith for forgiveness, nor is there in any of the religions outside the biblical tradition. By putting the gospel in terms of forgiveness, the church can raise an issue to which men must respond, one way or other — the issue of the nature of God and the problem of guilt. (This strategy will concern us in Chapter 5.)

In a word, what is the forgiveness announced by the gospel? It is the news that God has dealt effectively with those barriers which our failures have erected. It is the news that God does not wait in sublime patience until we achieve a minimum moral character, but that he refuses to allow our continued bankruptcy to stand between himself and us. The stories of Jesus' consorting with sinners are important, therefore, because in light of the resurrection they make the forgiving initiative of God clear, for Jesus did not tell men that when they were sufficiently reformed they might eat with him. The word of forgiveness, then, is the word that as far as God's receiving us as sons is concerned, our sins are irrelevant. Whoever refuses to believe this fact trudges inevitably through life with this accumulating burden on his back; conversely, the man who believes it discovers that he is free from this load and free to begin anew as an obedient citizen of God's kingdom.

Those who are familiar with Paul's thinking will recognize the fact that this understanding of forgiveness looks very much like his understanding of justification by faith — the belief that men are set in right relation (this is what "justification" means for Paul) by their trust in Jesus. Such a resemblance is not accidental, for it is clear that Paul generally avoids the word "forgiveness." Quite likely, he regarded justification by faith as the rationale of forgiveness; therefore he could point to the same reality with a different vocabulary. This is why the story of the forgiving father[7] (Luke 15:11-32) can be regarded as an excellent illustration of Paul's point.

The gospel of God's forgiveness, furthermore, is believable only if those who talk about it are actually forgiving other persons freely the way God has. The Lord's Prayer makes this fact clear, even if Matthew 18:23-35 does not. This means that the church which preaches God's forgiveness must also practice its own. In the last analysis, being forgiven by another person opens a window into the forgiving work of God more than anything else does. Forgiveness does not mean a condescending patience with other people's faults; such attitudes do not bring freedom, but intensify bondage. Rather, forgiveness means a steadfast refusal to treat another person on the basis of his actions, and a readiness to be his neighbor in spite of it. Such an attitude is possible when a person steadily bears in mind that he himself is treated in this way by God, and when he allows his own outlook to be transformed by this conviction. Here is precisely what repentance means, and why true repentance follows faith in God's initiative.

The first disciples found themselves constrained to live like pardoned criminals, forgiven debtors. Being forgiven led to the acts of the apostles, to forgiving acts by forgiven men. Their ability to develop a new mode of life was their day-to-day confirmation that they had really been forgiven. The second part of Jesus' parable said it must be like this. When we strip the old varnish off the idea of forgiveness and get down to the hardwood of the gospel, who can predict what the acts of modern apostles might be? Chapter 4 will show us what the first generation found itself doing, and this may give us a clue.

INSTEAD
OF CHRISTENDOM

Here we have no lasting city. . . .
—UNKNOWN CHRISTIAN WRITER
(Hebrews 13:14)

The church of Christ is a fellowship of pilgrims bound together by what is eternal and marching toward what is beyond history. And yet, all believers, all pilgrims in any time, have been molded and shaped by external circumstances much more effectively than they have ever realized. *

—JOSEPH L. HROMADKA

TEXT OF ACTS: 6:1-11:26 (omitting 7:1-53, the speech of Stephen)

THINGS TO LOOK FOR:

1. Read the entire section, noting the following divisions:
   A. The Hellenist controversy (6:1-8:3)
   B. The results of persecution (Philip, 8:4-40; Paul, 9:1-31)
   C. Peter's mission (9:32-11:18)
   D. The Antioch experiment (11:19-26)

2. This section reports how the church came to accept Gentiles. It sets the stage for the mission of Paul (reported in Chapter 13ff.). Bearing in mind the overall structure of Acts (see page 28), we see that Chapters 6-11 span the end of Part One and the beginning of Part Two. With the conversion of Paul, Part One ends. The stage is set: Philip has enlarged the concept of the church and the man who is to carry out the broadened mission has been converted. Part Two begins with the work of Peter, who inaugurated a new era when he baptized a Gentile. What Peter began under protest was carried out with enthusiasm by Paul. This thrust is the theme of Part Two.

3. The identity of the Hellenists has not yet been solved. We shall assume they are "Hellenizers" (as in "Judaizers") —Jews who live like Greeks. The problem reported in 6:1 arose out of communal life (see 2:43-47; 4:32-37). Notice that all seven men have Greek names. Tradition, not the text, labels these "deacons" (from the Greek *diakonos,* "servant" or "waiter").

4. Stephen's speech is a tirade against the temple and the Jews. It suggests that the charges against him (6:13f.) may not have been as false as Luke says. Stephen became the first witness to testify to the point of death ("martyr" means "witness").

5. This death brings two results: the work of Philip and the persecution by Paul (Saul).[1] Paul is eventually converted, and Acts reports the event three times: 9:1-30; 22:3-21; 26:2-23. These reports should be compared with Paul's own account in Galatians 1:11-24.

6. The careful construction of the Peter and Cornelius story and its basic repetition in 11:1-18 show that it is important for Luke. Note the sense of divine guidance here.

7. The Antioch church included Gentiles from the start. This became Paul's home church. It was here that the mission to Gentiles was born (13:1).

INSTEAD OF CHRISTENDOM

CHRISTENDOM IS NOT LIKE LAZARUS, WHO WAS RESTORED TO LIFE, but like Humpty Dumpty, who couldn't be put together again.

Studying Acts has led us to see not only where the first church was, but where ours is. Both live in a world without Christendom. Not only do we find ourselves outside the snug shelter of Christendom, of a culture which supported the church by its ideals and institutions, but we face a variety of non-Christian cultures in a way that has not been true for centuries. These include, among others, a strenuous Islam, a rejuvenated Buddhism, a militant Marxism, and an aggressive secularism. Moreover, the church faces all of these at the same time. Such is the situation in which we read Acts today.

But it is not enough simply to analyze the situation, nor to take inventory of the church's resources. A real danger is that the modern church will become expert in analysis but inept in action (the so-called "paralysis of analysis"). It may simply talk itself to death. The early church was different. This chapter shows how it acted on what it believed.

APOSTLES WITHOUT A KINGDOM

Although Luke doesn't say so, one may suspect that the disciples were disappointed when the Risen One told them they were to be witnessing apostles rather than administrators of a Christian Zionism. They did not really expect such a thing as the church turned out to be, nor were they prepared for the changes which the community of believers was to undergo. Like men of every period, the first believers did not act on the command of the Lord until the course of events compelled them to do so. We shall trace the story of how they did respond, beginning with the church's developing self-image.

Every congregation is in danger of having an inadequate image of itself and its work. How a congregation thinks of itself affects what it does. Here, for instance, is a common misconception of the church: "The church is an organization of like-minded people who get together for mutual support and to promote the cause of Christ." The trouble with such a definition is not that it is so wrong but that it is so inadequate. Obviously, the church *is* an organization, and its members *do* share a fairly common set of beliefs and it *does* try to promote the cause of Christ. But such a definition of the church can fit the Gideons just as well.

Acts can help us find a more adequate conception of the church and its work, because its author does not give us theories about the church but shows us what the church did. Acts, of course, does not tell us everything, but it is complete enough that we can infer how the early church thought of itself.

The starting-point in understanding the nature of the early church is the fact that all the first Christians were Jews. In fact, the church was born on a Jewish holiday, Pentecost.

If we could have interviewed the first Christians, they might have said something like this: "We are the true Israel, because we know who the Messiah is. The old Israel, which is now scattered around the world, is being called to confess that the Messiah is Jesus. This is our mission — to summon Israel to this confession. Because we are the true Israel, all God's promises in the Bible refer to us; in Jesus and in us are fulfilled all of God's commitments to his people. We express this fulfillment by perfectly faithful obedience to the will of God in the Law of Moses, the Torah. For this reason we are in the temple every day, worshiping and thanking God for sending the Messiah, praying that all Israel may see that he has come in Jesus."

Some of the early Christians in Jerusalem gained a reputation for a puritanical piety. James, the brother of Jesus, came to be described as follows:

> He was called the 'Just' by all men from the Lord's time to ours [a century later]. . . . He drank no wine or strong drink, nor did he eat flesh; no razor went upon his head; he did not anoint himself with oil, and he did not go to the baths. . . . He used to enter alone into the temple and be found kneeling and praying for forgiveness for the people, so that his knees grew hard like a camel's because of his constant worship of God. . . .[2]

Even if this account is partly legendary, it nevertheless reflects the outlook of main-line Jerusalem Christianity. It was a devout, disciplined Judaism centered in the belief that Jesus was the Messiah. The Messiah's people, of course, were the final Israel.

The people who believed in Jesus were not the only ones claiming to be the true, final Israel. One of the things that characterized Jewish religion at this time is the fact that there were competing groups, each of which claimed to be the bearer of the true faith. In other words, the pluralistic situation which has come upon the American scene is not new to the church at all. The church was born into a pluralistic setting. Pluralism is not new, but is native to the church.

The most famous group which claimed to be the true Israel was the Essenes, who probably wrote the so-called Dead Sea Scrolls. They were like some extreme present-day sect which might withdraw to Death Valley, getting ready for Armageddon in America. In addition, there were the Pharisees. Like the Essenes, they centered faith and life in the Law of Moses, but, unlike the Essenes, they were more tolerant, less narrow. They interpreted the commands of the Bible by spelling out specific laws so that every person would know precisely what God's will was. Their regulations became very detailed. The Pharisee took God's will so seriously that he wanted to know whether eating an egg laid on the Sabbath did or did not violate the Commandment. The central institution of the Pharisees was the synagogue, a combination of church and school. Another group was the Sadducees. These were largely-aristocratic priestly families who were concerned to preserve the temple and its worship. They regarded only the first five books of the Bible as Scripture, and opposed both the Pharisees and Essenes. In order to preserve the temple ritual, they cooperated with the Roman occupation army; therefore they were hated by extreme patriots, the Zealots. The Zealots were Jewish "freedom fighters" who led the great revolt against Rome in A.D. 66. In addition, there were also the followers of John the Baptist as well as other baptizing sects around the Jordan River. Moreover, this entire web of Jewish "denominations" quarreled with the Samaritans, who lived in a district north of Jerusalem. The Samaritans and Jews had hated one another for centuries because each claimed to be the true descendants of the Israelites who had settled in Palestine.

In other words, Christianity was born into a situation of tension and rivalry. All pictures of New Testament Palestine as a peaceful land peopled by humble psalm-singing shepherds or devout farmers murmuring prayers as they scratched a living from the soil are far too closely manicured to be of help. The devout were there, to be sure; but bitter controversy over which form of devoutness was willed by God was there too. Precisely because each group insisted it was expressing God's will, the controversies were fierce and the loyalties deep. Each group developed a style of life which expressed its faith. Since Judaism has always been more concerned about styles of life than sets of ideas, these groups could agree on basic ideas. They disagreed violently, however, over the way of life which they believed to be the appropriate and God-willed outcome of those beliefs. Therefore, anyone who abandoned one of the traditional alternatives, in order to accept Jesus as the Messiah and to join the Christian "Way," [3] had to have clear reasons for doing so. He not only adopted different ideas but entered upon a particular style of life at the same time.

The most famous feature of early Christian life was the experiment in communal living. This is sometimes called early Christian communism. Actually, this term is not a good description of it, because the people shared only the wealth they already had, and not the means of producing more. We ought to call it "communalism." They pooled their resources and lived out a common fund (Acts 2:44-46; 4:32-37).

Acts does not tell us why the early Christians developed this kind of life together. There were probably a number of reasons, among which we may mention six: (1) Jesus himself had spoken harsh words about wealth and had blessed the poor. Matthew reports that Jesus said, "Blessed are the poor in spirit," but Luke's version is probably more correct: "Blessed are you poor" (Matthew 5:3; Luke 6:20). (2) They found themselves united by faith in Jesus. Such a brotherhood might view private possessions as causing distinctions that had no place within their group. (3) Such ideas were in the air at the time. The Old Testament has a long tradition of regarding the pious poor as the specially devout. Besides, the Essenes at the Dead Sea apparently shared wealth and practiced a communistic life,[4] as did other groups at the time. Sharing wealth may have seemed the natural thing to do. (4) They expected the Son of Man, the cosmic Judge, to appear soon. In such a situation, there was no point in clinging to private possessions. People expecting the end of the world have often "sold out" — only to be forced to buy everything back. (5) The early church seems to have celebrated the Lord's Supper as part of a general common meal. Originally, the Lord's Supper and the church supper were one and the same occasion. A further step was the sharing of all meals. (6) The early church included a number of Galileans who had moved to Jerusalem; taking care of them may have led to a common fund for all members of the brotherhood.

Acts is just as silent about the future of this practice as about its origin, but apparently the idea did not last, nor was it transplanted to other congregations. But it has cropped out again and again in the history of the church. The most common examples are the monasteries right up to our own time; also there are the Hutterites in South Dakota, Canada, and Uruguay; and the interracial community known as Koinonia Farm, in Georgia. We may not agree that the sharing of property is essential to being a follower of Jesus; but, on the other hand, there is something sick about the speed with which we over-caloried, capitalist Christians hasten to reassure ourselves that this early Christian community had no communism and furthermore that its way of life never really worked. At least, these people saw the need to translate convictions into something concrete. Again and again, Acts refers to the first believers as "those of the Way" — that is, those who developed an actual style of life based on faith in Jesus.

But in any case, at the outset, it was a Jewish Way in the name of the Messiah Jesus. The apostles were without a kingdom to govern, without a Christendom to administer, but they were not without a way of life.

CROSSING THE FRONTIER

The early believers not only stood on the frontier of faith when they confronted other kinds of life within Judaism, but soon found themselves on a frontier *within* the church. The question soon arose whether faith in Jesus required *one* particular style of life or permitted a variety.

The story begins with the sudden appearance of the Hellenists (6:1). These were the liberal Jews who had adopted Greek ways. Ever since the armies of Alexander the Great had swept back the Persians, there had been Jews in Palestine who lived like Greeks. They spoke Greek, dressed like Greeks, shaved their beards, participated in sports, and read the Bible in Greek. In Jerusalem, there were synagogues for such Greek-living Jews. In the time of Jesus, this Greek element was clearly present (especially in Galilee), right beside others who emphasized the Hebraic traditions of Jewish life. Some of these Greek-living Jews became Christians, and naturally brought their ways of living into the church with them. Consequently, there were now two kinds of Christians, both believing in Jesus but believing with different words and living different kinds of lives. This division is what seems to lie behind the short references in Acts.[5]

When the Hellenist widows (that is, widows of Hellenized Jews) complained that they were neglected in the distribution of food from the common fund, Luke says the church appointed seven Hellenists to manage this work for the entire church, while the apostles did the preaching and teaching. The details are not at all clear,[6] because the only thing we read about the seven men is that they were doing exactly what the apostles had done. But what Luke wants to say through this story is fairly clear — that the church learned how to agree to disagree in such matters, that it learned to live with two modes of life because both were transcended by a common faith. In other words, Luke shows that the church learned not to insist on particular customs and cultural patterns. This was a decisive lesson.

The stoning of Stephen had a double result: Paul persecuted the believers, and the Hellenists left town. But the Hellenists did not become simply the first Christian refugees; they became missionaries as well. And thus the Jerusalem church found itself on a frontier it had not expected. How the church crossed this frontier is the story Luke wants to tell. He tells it first through the Hellenists, and then through Peter and Paul. In this chapter, we will leave Paul aside.

Philip, the refugee, dared to convert Samaritans. To grasp the meaning of his boldness, we must remember the bitterness between Jews and Samaritans. Besides the years of hate, there were theological differences too. For one thing, the Samaritans accepted as Scripture only the Pentateuch (just as the Jewish Sadducees did), but they had their own version of it. However, the Samaritans hated the Sadducees because Samaritans regarded the Jerusalem temple as illegitimate (this fact is reflected in the Samaritan woman's words to Jesus in John 4:20f.). Moreover, the Samaritans expected a messiah of their own, a prophet like Moses who could restore all things (as the Samaritan woman reminds Jesus in John 4:25f.).

In this light, Acts significantly says that Philip preached Christ — that is, he preached the Messiah. To summon Samaritans to believe in a Jewish messiah was to invite them to forego their own hope. They were to see in the Jew Jesus the real fulfillment of their hopes along with those of the Jews! By preaching Jesus as the Messiah to the Samaritans, Philip was trying to bridge the gap between the religious hopes of these two quarreling peoples.

For the Samaritans who believed and were baptized, the gap was closed. The reason is obvious: Believers in one Messiah are members of one messianic community; they have no longer a basis for excluding each other. Faith in Jesus as the Messiah is stronger than allegiance to custom and local religion. Philip could take such a forward step because as a Hellenist he had already seen that a person's faith in Jesus transcended Jewish customs. He himself was a Greek-living Jew who believed in Jesus just as much as a Jewish-living Jew did. The inner logic of this fact drove him to see that faith and custom must be distinguished from one another. The fact that faith produces *a* style of life does not mean that it must produce only *one* style of life. Hence, Philip saw that a Samaritan could believe in Jesus and still be a Samaritan. With this new insight, he crossed the cultural frontier and summoned the church to follow him.

When news of Philip's work trickled back to Jerusalem, the congregation was flabbergasted. But they were not overwhelmed. They dispatched two men, Peter and John, to investigate and to make sure that this new church would be properly constituted and made legitimate. When they arrived, they communicated the Holy Spirit by the laying on of hands. Although this understanding of the Spirit makes us nervous, it is clear that the apostles accepted the new group of believers on a par with themselves, and demonstrated their trust by insisting that this new congregation was to have exactly the same divine empowering as the home church in Jerusalem. This was to be the Christian Church in Samaria and not simply a Samaritan church. The old cleavages were not to be perpetuated in the New Israel. Through Philip the church's mission to all Israel took the next step: an attempt to reconstitute Israel (including the Samaritans) on the basis of faith in Jesus alone, rather than on the basis of the culture and customs of Judaism.

This was the church's first significant encounter with discrimination and racism. It did not flee. Nor did it wait for the Samaritans to petition Pontius Pilate for equal rights within the Jerusalem church. Instead, the church acted on the logic of the gospel and welcomed the Samaritans as brothers in Christ. Equally important, perhaps, is the fact that, as the apostles returned to Jerusalem, they themselves preached to the Samaritans. The church was beginning to follow Philip.

The second story of Philip concerns the Ethiopian who was returning from a pilgrimage to Jerusalem. This person (a eunuch, in keeping with ancient customs for imperial servants) was a Gentile, a Negro. This unnamed, emasculated

Negro is accorded a special place in Luke's story because he represents the Gentiles who had become deeply interested in Judaism. In this period in Jewish history, there was an intensive effort to convert the pagans to the faith of Israel.[7] Many were converted and circumcised (and probably baptized), thus becoming full members of the Jewish communities. These were known as proselytes. Others held back because they refused circumcision and the Jewish way of life but were willing to accept the religious beliefs and morals. To grasp the pungency of Luke's story, we must remember that according to the Bible no eunuch could become a proselyte (Deuteronomy 23:1f.). We must also remember that Isaiah 56 promised that in the Era of Fulfillment, the eunuch would not be excluded. In fact, a large part of that chapter concerns the foreigner's place among the people of God in the great age to come.

Luke reports that the eunuch was reading the Bible, presumably in Greek, while riding along. Since it was the practice in ancient times to read aloud, Philip was able to identify the exact passage the Ethiopian was reading — Isaiah 53, which describes the Servant of God who would suffer to redeem the nations. This scene provided Philip with just the opportunity he needed, and so he volunteered to interpret the passage. Luke puts it this way: "Beginning with this Scripture, he 'gospeled' Jesus to him" (my translation). Convinced by the message, the man stopped the chariot near a pool and was baptized then and there. Thus a second step was taken in the crossing of the frontier.

Luke's story carries two points: (1) Through the fact that the Ethiopian was a eunuch, Philip continued to express the conviction of the early church that the new age had already dawned; and the promises of God were therefore being fulfilled in the church. (2) By the circumstance that the eunuch was an Ethiopian, Philip also showed that the boundaries of the church were not limited to Judaism, nor even to the borders of the Israel of the Old Testament which had included Samaria. Moreover, not even those whom the Bible excluded from Judaism were obliged to remain outside the church if they believed in Jesus. On this decisive point everything hinged. God's people in the age of fulfillment was being constituted, Luke shows, on the basis of faith in Jesus, and on this basis alone.

Whereas Philip crossed the frontier alone, Peter started to lead the church across it. Not only did he approve of Philip's work in Samaria, but he himself converted a Roman army officer, Cornelius. Luke regards this event as the decisive turning-point, and therefore puts it near the beginning of his central section as an appropriate introduction. It is the most detailed of the "frontier stories," and is repeated in Chapter 11 to drive home the point. The heart of the matter is put at the end: "Then to the Gentiles also God has granted repentance unto life." [8] That is, God himself has nudged us across the frontier and has made it clear that Gentiles may be part of God's people and remain Gentiles at the same time. Since Luke's interests in the story are most clearly revealed in 11:1-18, we will follow this account.

Here we see the breakthrough toward evangelizing Gentiles. But we note that the criticism leveled against Peter was not for talking to the Gentiles about Jesus but for eating with them (11:3). To put it into modern terms, the Jerusalem congregation had no serious objections to Gentiles' believing in Jesus, so long as they "kept their place." What the traditionalists could not see and would not tolerate was the idea that Peter was ignoring the customs of segregation between Jew and pagan.[9] To the Jerusalem conservatives this act was unnecessary and unwarranted. So Peter was called on the carpet.

For this reason the story emphasizes Peter's vision of the things which Jews were not permitted to eat. Thus the problem of segregation is accented in the middle of a story about converting Gentiles. The reason Luke makes this point is that for him these themes are closely related. By putting the question of segregated eating into a setting of international evangelism, Luke shows that one cannot really preach Christ to any man with whom one is not willing to eat. In other words, what God has cleansed, no man may call unclean. If God has called pork, for example, clean and fit to eat, Peter has no right to insist that it is unclean; he may not refuse to eat it on these grounds, even though the Bible forbids him to do so. In exactly the same way, the argument implies, if God has now called the Gentiles "clean," Peter has no basis for refusing to associate with them. But has God actually done this?

The whole point of the visions and other elements of the story is that God himself has made this point clear. Luke hammers on this theme again and again as he recounts the visions of Cornelius and Peter, the work of the Spirit in telling Peter to go to Caesarea, and the coming of the Spirit before Cornelius was baptized. These incidents are told to show how God was nudging Peter across the barrier. The leading player in this drama is not Peter but God; therefore the church has no real alternative. Peter ends his report to the church by saying, "Who was I that I could withstand God?"

The opposition was silenced. But this was not all, for theirs could have been a glum silence. Luke goes on to say that they "glorified God" — that is, they were grateful to him for making it clear that the Jews and Gentiles no longer had any significant barrier between them, though their customs continued to differ. Both groups had the opportunity to repent. Jew and Gentile were united in their common status before God, and, for seeing this fact, they gave God glory.

The history of Jewish Christianity shows that either Luke idealized this new enthusiasm or the church soon lapsed into old ways of thinking. Probably both conclusions are valid. In fact, even the Gentile church, *our* church, has slipped so far back that eleven o'clock on Sunday morning is still the most segregated hour of the week. Like the Jerusalem conservatives, many American congregations are willing to convert the Africans but not willing to worship and eat with Negroes. For exactly the same reason, Will Campbell has observed that if the church were to solve the problem of segregation in our generation, we will have made so much progress that we will be precisely where we started.[10]

The story of how the church crossed the cultural frontier has still another part. It is the story of the Hellenist refugees who left Palestine altogether. Some fled north to Syria, as far as the great city of Antioch. Here they developed the most daring experiment of all: an interracial church. This was the first such congregation. The Jerusalem church was disturbed by such an adventure. It was one thing to make concessions for a man like Cornelius; after all, he was a Roman officer. But here was a whole congregation experimenting with the meaning of the gospel. So they dispatched Barnabas to set matters straight. When he arrived, however, he liked what he saw, and went to Tarsus to find Paul. Together they returned to lead this exciting new church.

It was in this Antioch congregation that the believers were first called "Christians." Significantly, they were not known as "Jesusite" Jews; rather, since they were united by their worship of Jesus as Christ, outsiders dubbed them "Christians." This name shows that the church had discovered that its real center lay in its confession of faith (Jesus as the Christ) and not in the customs and cultures of the members. It is not accidental that, precisely in such a church as this, people heard the Spirit's summons to mission in the whole Gentile world. This congregation had passed the frontier.

The Church without the Messiah

We have seen that the story of how the church came to accept Gentile members on a par with Jewish believers is really the story of how it transcended the cultural borders of the faith. In this issue Acts presents us with a precedent, a pace-setting example of the church living without its "Christendom." Perhaps the point will be sharper if we pose a question: What is the appropriate relation between the church and the cultures in which it finds itself? If "culture" is too technical a word, we can discuss many of the same problems by using a popular substitute, "a way of life" ("culture" is a more inclusive term). Thus the issue becomes: What is the appropriate relationship between the church and particular ways of life? between the church and the American way of life? the Burmese way of life? the Congolese? the Soviet?

Whoever has seen a bearded, black-garbed Amish Mennonite hitching his horse and buggy to a parking meter has seen one sect's clear solution to the problem of church and culture. During the formative years of this Anabaptist group's history, they committed themselves to plain things as an appropriate protest against the display of wealth and finery. Hence, as the Christian way of life, they emphasized plain clothes in somber colors, hooks and eyes instead of fancy buttons, and rural life instead of mercantile values. Once the group had agreed that such was the appropriate way for a Christian to live (anything else being regarded as worldly), they tried to freeze the pattern for all time. For the faithful, these customs, these folkways, these habits of dress and speech all make up the Christian way of life. For the Hutterian Brethren, the accepted way includes a shared economy as well. For such persons, it is inconceivable that Christians could live any other way and be "good Christians" at the same time. Conversion to Christian faith, for them, includes conversion to this kind of life.

The Amish relationship to modern society shows us a perennial problem in strong outline. The whole church faces the same issue wherever the church goes, and whenever it is sensitive. It faces the question now when an African must

decide what to do with his three wives when he becomes a
Christian; it faced it long ago in deciding what to do with the
pagan holy day, December 25; still farther in the past it began
to see the issue when the Hellenist Jews professed their faith
in Jesus. The issue is always the same: What does Christ do
to customs? What customs does Christ require of his followers?
What is the relation of Christ to culture?

The issue is particularly sharp because it has two prongs.
On one side, the Christian faith must express itself in particular practices. It must develop a style of life consistent
with its belief or evaporate. The instinct of the Amish people
was sterling-sound when it required the Anabaptist convictions to jell into a mode of life that was consistent with those
convictions. The first congregation in Jerusalem likewise developed a way of life which rang true to its faith. For the
Amish it was plain living on a farm; for the Jerusalem believers it was a completely shared life. In both cases, faith
developed a specific, recognizable expression. As my former
colleague, Professor Denbeaux of Wellesley College, used to
say, "Faith must become something or it becomes nothing."
One danger of modern Christianity (especially in certain
emphases of its evangelism) is that its faith may be so much
a matter of the heart that it evaporates in the hand. When
this happens, there is no Christian alternative to modern life
at all.

The other prong of the problem is the fact that even though
faith expresses itself in a particular style of life, in a concrete
cultural form, this expression is not absolute. This point was
quite difficult for the first believers to accept, and for the
Amish as well. The first believers, however, did learn it, because they apparently did not insist that every congregation
live a shared life. They did not require this particular expression of Christianity. This lesson was the first step. The second
came when they realized that a Jew could believe in Jesus as
the Messiah without abandoning his Greek ways of living. The

third lesson was learned when they came to see that even a Gentile could believe in Jesus as Christ and know the presence of God's Spirit and yet remain a Gentile altogether. These lessons were not easy to learn, and the passing of the centuries has not made them easier for us.

The issue can be stated as a proposition: Wherever the gospel goes, believers must develop a Christian style of life with roots in the cultural soil. Believers in Britain, Burma, and Bolivia will therefore develop different kinds of cultures and customs in the name of Christ. At the same time, neither the British, nor the Burman, nor the Bolivian Christians may assume that theirs is the only true Christian style of life. The Christian faith may reshape all customs without being identified with any of them, because it transcends all of them.

On the most elemental level, this idea suggests missionary strategy in simple things. For example, converts in Japan may be encouraged to praise God with native Japanese music instead of Bach's chorales or Homer Rodeheaver's gospel songs. But far more is required than this: It is the freedom and responsibility of every Christian community, in whatever culture it finds itself, to discover what it means to be Christian *in that place* and to develop a kind of life consistent with the faith *in that place*. It is not only inevitable, but essential, that there be differences among Christians in matters of custom and culture. It is equally essential (though unfortunately it has not always been equally inevitable) that such differing Christians recognize their unity in faith, and so accept each other as brothers in Christ though aliens in culture and race.

This acceptance has never been easy, nor it is today. That we have not simply been toying with a theory but probing a reality can be seen by looking at Christians in America. It was no easier for the Christian Jew to eat with Gentile believers than it is for some Christian whites to eat with Christian Negroes at the Lord's table (or at the drugstore, for that matter!). The first church managed to desegregate itself because the logic of the gospel required this action.[11] Step by step this church was led to see that witnessing to the resurrection of Jesus had consequences for customs and cultural tensions. Its members saw that witnessing to the resurrection of Jesus meant bearing witness to *his* lordship over all customs and to *their* own transformation within them at the same time. They also saw that this meant bearing witness to the power of the risen Jesus to transform their attitudes and to transcend the barriers of culture and race. They saw, too, that the power of the resurrection was not simply the power that took Jesus from the tomb in the garden to the throne in heaven but is also the power that transformed the believers into brothers of every believer, regardless of the culture in which he did his believing and his living. Wherever the church insists on being apostolic, it must follow the apostles here, in the ordering of its life and not simply in the ordination of its leaders.

We have mentioned the possibility that every culture may be Christianized (that is, may receive the impact of the gospel in particular customs) in its own way. This brings us to a further question. Suppose a culture, a civilization, a society bases its life and ideals on Christianity. What is the destiny of a culture that has been basically Christian? This is the fundamental problem of our own civilization, for it is the question of the nature and destiny of what was Christendom.

There is no doubt that there has been such a thing as a Christian civilization in the North Atlantic community. The fact that the penetration of the gospel has often been only skin deep is not decisive for our question. What is decisive is that for centuries, from Caesar Constantine in the fourth to Kaiser Wilhelm in the twentieth, Christianity set the standards for European civilization. When standards were considered to be violated, they were Christian standards and not pagan or Moslem ones. Christopher Dawson[12] has correctly pointed out that Christianity is as basic to European civilization as Islam is to the Arabian or Confucianism to the Chinese. Christianity made a really European civilization possible, and we should be thankful for it.

But Christian dominance of the culture is not an unmixed blessing nor one without dangers. It was bought at a terrible price, by which Christianity became the tribal religion which blessed the chiefs of Europe as they warred on fellow believers, expelled Jews from one country after another, crusaded against infidel Turks, and persecuted heretic Christians. Moreover, when the Christian missionary moved into the new worlds across newly-charted seas, he assumed that becoming a Christian meant becoming a Western man, just as the Jerusalem church believed that becoming a Christian meant becoming a Jew. Symbols of this identification of Christ and culture in an earlier day were the Mother Hubbard dress and the missionary compound. Here was a Christian outpost in a pagan wilderness, a place where the white man's religion and his insecticide went hand in hand. We should not be surprised that there came to be "rice Christians," persons converted for the sake of cultural and economic advantages.

Nevertheless, no culture has yet succeeded in becoming so Christian that it can say: "The kingdoms of this world have become the kingdoms of our Christ."[18] In other words, the church lives in the West which is more or less Christianized (that is, reflects Christian impact on morals, art, attitudes, etc.), but it lives always without the Messiah enthroned in "Jerusalem." The half-Christianized civilizations in which we find ourselves remind us that the Messiah is not here, and that the church works and waits. The coming of the Messiah will bring the Messianic Age. The Messianic Age means a messianic culture, a civilization which is totally redeemed, which is totally under the lordship of the Messiah, which no longer has pockets of resistance. Only then will the Christian community be identical with civilization as a whole. Only then will there be a consummated Christendom. In the meantime, no culture, no civilization, no Christendom is really messianic, even if it bears the imprint of the Messiah Jesus. The belief in the "Second Coming of Christ" (not a New Testament phrase!) is valuable as a symbol of this fact about Christianity in history. Grasping this basic theological point does not require one to insist that the Second Coming means the arrival of Jesus as a man from outer space.

Because the church lives and works without the Messiah, it must distinguish between western Christianized culture and the gospel itself. Never may it confuse them in its evangelistic work! Every cultural imperialism in the name of the Messiah (every attempt to make Western men out of Asian converts) is a betrayal of the hope for the Messianic Age and an idolization of one's own culture. If the church does not transcend every cultural situation, it will confuse itself with the kingdom of God.

Paul reminds us that our citizenship is in heaven (Philippians 3:20) and not simply in our own nation. Many find themselves assuming that being a "good American" is the same thing as being a good Christian and is as close to being in heaven as is possible on earth. In fact, many Americans are so satisfied with the American Way of Life that, if they can afford all its benefits here, they see little reason to act as citizens of heaven.

Paul does not remind the Philippians of their transcendent allegiance in order to take their minds off the problems of hammering out a Christian style of life in Philippi. Actually, he reminds them of this transcendent citizenship in order to provide them with a fixed point by which to chart their course. As sailors have known for centuries, ships on earth are steered according to stars in the heavens. Likewise, knowing that their citizenship is in heaven, Christians are free to build a Christian form of life that makes sense wherever their homeland is. Thus, American Christians are free to build a Christian style of life on the American scene if they remember that, in the last analysis, America is not "God's country" any more than the Ukraine is; and that, whatever cultural achievements Americans may build, they build as pilgrims dwelling in huts, temporary shelters.

For each culture, each nation, each society to be shaped by the gospel in its own peculiar way requires that, first of all, it hear the good news in its own terms. This requirement is the problem of the next chapter.

CHAPTER FIVE

MEETING
ANOTHER FAITH

We also are men, of like nature with you, and bring you good news, that you should turn from these vain things to a living God. . . .
—St. Paul (Acts 14:15)

Theology, the interpretative rethinking of the Biblical revelation, cannot seek for reconciliation with philosophy, but should seek for interaction and communication with it.*
—Hendrik Kraemer

We do not believe in any possibility of an ideological synthesis of communism and Christian faith. . . . However, a new atmosphere may be created, an atmosphere of a right struggle *for man, his dignity and integrity.***
—Joseph L. Hromadka

. . . modern man's cultural ideals, values, meanings . . . are the necessary . . . springboard, "available past," for understanding the Gospel today. Does the modern scientifically-minded agnostic, who holds on to some sort of sense in the existing collapse of meaning . . . have to be disillusioned . . . before he can grasp the Gospel? Does he have to be thrown back to zero . . . ?***
—Amos Wilder

THE TEXT OF ACTS: 13:13-52; 17:16-34

THINGS TO LOOK FOR:

1. These passages swirl us into the stream of Paul's travels (a map is helpful here). One is from the so-called "First Missionary Journey" (it is doubtful that Paul numbered them), and the other is from the "Second."

2. Because the story of Paul in Antioch of Pisidia (in Asia Minor, southwest of modern Ankara, Turkey) is so detailed, it must have had special importance for Luke. Paul participates in the service according to custom. Note the themes of the sermon. The pronouncement in 13:46 does not mark a shift in Paul's strategy, for he continues to go first to the Jews. Rather it is a general announcement about the gospel: Because the Jews rejected it, it was received by the Gentiles. This sermon and its setting are used by Luke as symbols of the church's experience; it accounts for the fact that the church is more Gentile than Jewish, even though it is founded on the Messiah Jesus.

3. In Acts 17, Paul is in Greece. Thessalonica is modern Salonika. From here Paul traveled down the peninsula to Athens. From here he went to Corinth where he stayed at least a year and a half (18: 1-17). We learn almost nothing about his long stay, a fact which constantly frustrates our efforts to understand his letters to this church. In contrast, the brief stay in Athens is told in detail, again with special emphasis on the speech. Obviously, this setting and speech must be important for Luke, more important than Corinth. (Because of the Corinthian letters, *we* regard the stay in Corinth as more important.) In fact, the sermon in the synagogue and the speech on Mars Hill are the only examples of Paul's missionary preaching which Luke provides us. This is why these sections are so important for Luke's picture of Paul.

4. The scene in Athens merits special attention because here Paul addresses the Gentile world on a high level. Note how the story is put together: Verses 16-21 set the stage (note the kind of results Paul has had); 22-31 give the address itself; 32-34 report the result. Observe the point at which Paul is interrupted. Why was he forced to stop here?

5. The speech divides into a framework and a core. The framework is 22-23 and 30-31. It deals with the theme of worship-without-understanding. The core is a critique of Athenian religion and theology. Note what is said about God and man. Why does Paul quote Greek writers (Epimenides and Aratus) but not the Bible? According to this speech, what is wrong with making statues of God?

6. Paul's attitude reported here must be compared with his own statements in Romans 1:18-32. Why does Paul deal so much more severely with pagan religion in Romans than in Acts? Is one more true to **Paul than the other? Why or why not?**

MEETING ANOTHER FAITH

"For the first time since the Constantine victory in A.D. 312 and its consequences, the Christian Church is heading toward a real and spiritual encounter with the great non-Christian religions."[1] So writes Hendrik Kraemer, who has spent his life dealing with the problem.

Two modern developments have brought about this new encounter. (1) The disintegration of Christendom means that Europe and America are mission fields in which the church faces another faith — secularism, a non-religious understanding of man. (2) In our shrunken world, Christian and Moslem, Buddhist and Hindu live cheek to jowl. Even though Christians once conducted military crusades against the "infidel" Turks and more recently by missionary activity have tried to rescue men from other faiths regarded as virtually pure darkness, Kraemer is right: ". . . a real meeting in openness and fairness has never yet taken place."

Today, however, Christians face other faiths in all parts of the world, including Europe and America. This meeting with other religions does not occur only in libraries or secluded places where uninterrupted, objective discussion can proceed. Mostly, it takes place wherever a Christian with integrity and sensitivity finds himself. It may be the Christian in Kenya who faces the demands and dangers of relating his life to that of a newly liberated nation, or a believer in

Burma who is surrounded by a revitalized Buddhism, or the follower of Jesus in Czechoslovakia who is challenged by a Marxist version of salvation and society; it may be the Christian merchant in America facing vigorous commercial challenges to Christian faith. Wherever it is, the confrontation with the non-Christian faiths is under way. Because this encounter will accelerate, we must know what we are about and how we are to proceed.

NOT NEW BUT NATIVE

Again and again we come back to the basic fact that we are no longer in a Christendom in which we may take the Christian faith for granted, but in a worldwide pluralism where Christianity is a minority. This situation has important consequences for the work of the church. If we were still in Christendom, we could look on our task as simply translation — that is, of finding ways to tell "the natives" or "the outsiders" what we believe. We must not underestimate the importance of such translation on every level of the church's work, whether it be the heroic efforts of missionary translators compiling word lists in the jungles or the sophisticated efforts to translate Christian concepts into the idiom of university students.[2] Good translation is an absolute minimum, whether it be literal translation of the Bible or, in a broader sense, the restatement of Christian faith. For witnessing without Christendom, however, translation alone is not enough; simply *saying* over again what the church has believed will not suffice. In our day, we must be prepared to *interpret* the gospel, to demonstrate its rationale to the inquirer and its concretion to the observer.

This is not all. Christendom not only has collapsed around us but has dissolved within us — *within us Christians as well.* There are many people generally involved with Christianity who simply do not know what it is to which they are committed. Some are committed to a vague kind of belief in God and goodness as taught by Jesus, and others are tied to a packaged "plan of salvation." Both groups need to discover the dynamics of believing in the living God who is made known in Jesus' death and resurrection.

In other words, it is true that the encounter between the Christian faith and a competing allegiance occurs "on the mission field," but in our day this field is not only in the Congo jungle and the American suburb, but in the Christian soul as well. The modern Christian meets another faith within his own heart. Not only has the security of cultural Christianity disintegrated on the outside but it has evaporated on the inside also. Hence, one does not become a Christian by default, but only by decision. In a sense, this decision has always been required; today, however, we see the crisis more sharply than before.

This problem is often painfully clear in theological students. One reason a modern theological education brings so much agony to the students is that they find the ramparts of faith on which they thought they were standing to be really the ruins of Christendom, and that the gospel actually summons them to a radical kind of faith for which they are scarcely prepared. They are in agony because no one has told them that believing and preaching the gospel in a world without Christendom means literally risking their lives. None of the things they had taken for granted, such as the authority of the Bible, the absoluteness of the gospel, the meaning of Jesus, and the work of the church can be taken for granted today, but must be avowed as decisions of faith. Students are pained because, in our day, learning more about the Bible, theology, Jesus, and the church does not make it easier for them to believe, but actually defines the borderline on which they must be willing to make a commitment in faith. The sooner the church as a whole understands this frontier, the sooner can its ministers deal honestly with the issues of faith and doubt in today's world.

If the realities of our situation are startlingly new to our generation, they are not new to the church. In fact, they are its native soil. We have already seen that the Palestinian church confronted rivals who also claimed to be the true Israel. Taking the gospel to the Gentiles compounded this problem, for now there was not simply the Jewish pluralism but the pagan pluralism to deal with as well. Acts does not discuss this challenge, but takes it for granted and shows how the church worked in such circumstances. Looking more closely at the situation reflected in Acts will illumine our own tasks and opportunities. Luke shows us Paul, who, as missionary theologian, spent his career grappling with such issues.

Paul has been made into such a super-apostle that we find it hard to see him as he really was. Before viewing him as a theologian or Christian pastor, we should recognize Paul as a figure of the ancient world in general. Seen historically, Paul's mission as a wandering preacher was neither new nor unusual. To his world he was simply one more traveling preacher of some religion or other. The ancient world had been full of such men for two hundred years. These wandering preachers often took advantage of their situation and became "beatniks" who prided themselves on not working or washing. Some came to preach and became panhandlers. Later, wandering Christian prophets did the same thing. Second and Third John reflect such problems. Elmer Gantry is not really an American invention, only an American version of a timeless personality. Historically, Paul's itinerant ministry must be seen against this background.

Luke shows us two aspects of Paul's work. One is his pattern of inaugurating his work in the synagogues. Here was not only the logical starting point for a Jewish Christian but the theological starting point as well, for the core of the message to the Jews has always centered in the messiahship of Jesus, wherein Jesus brings the meaning of Israel to a head.

Paul himself insisted on the paradox that, although the gospel was received on exactly the same terms by Jews and Gentiles, salvation was nonetheless "to the Jew first" (Romans 1:16f). Luke provides his readers with a classic example of Paul's synagogue preaching in Acts 13. The second thing Luke shows about Paul's work is that he preached to Gentiles in various places. Especially interesting is the comment that in Ephesus he rented a hall for daily lectures (Acts 19:9). Paul's presentation of the gospel to Gentiles called for a different approach from his mission to the Jews. This can be seen clearly in Acts 17, the story of Paul in Athens.

Acts reports that, when Paul strolled through the streets of Athens, he was impressed by the abundance of religions. He probably had an impression of Athenian religion similar to our own reaction when we look at the church ads in a city paper. No one in the ancient world was waiting for an apostle to offer him something to believe. Like our own cities, those of the ancient world offered a bewildering assortment of religious cults and beliefs. Precisely this fact raises the perennial problem for preachers in pluralistic settings: How does one communicate the gospel in a world already full of competing religions? Our problem was Paul's problem too; our situation is not new at all, but native to the Christian church.

Luke's portrait of Paul will come into focus better if we note briefly the major alternatives to the Christian faith which Paul faced. We cannot, of course, describe in detail the religions of the Roman empire, but we must be content to outline the situation. Basically, we may distinguish between the religions of the state and those of personal salvation. We will consider the religions of the state in the next chapter; here we focus on these religions which offered avenues to salvation: popular philosophy, saving knowledge, and transforming ritual. Each had a "gospel" for the Athenians.

1. The popular philosophy was Stoicism, which was more a movement than a system of ideas dominated by one teacher.

Three elements of the Stoic gospel merit attention. *First*, the Stoics believed that the universe (and everything in it) was ruled by Law, and that this Law was reasonable and intelligible. Man, who is a miniature universe, is also ruled by this Law. Man knows that this fact is so, because this reasonable Law resides in him and determines his thinking. It is called the Logos (this term can be translated "word," as in John 1:1) or reason. Because the universe operates according to the Logos, this Logos is the Law of the cosmos and the Law of man as well. *Second*, since everything is governed by Law (Logos), man lives in a closed world, a world of cause and effect, a world in which everything works like an oiled machine. This harmonious working of the universe is the result of Providence (a word Christians borrowed from Stoics). Consequently, in this philosophy, everything that happens according to the Logos is not only according to nature but is really for the best. Hence, they said that man ought to accept his destiny, attuning himself to the universe, for in the last analysis there is no alternative anyway. *Third*, man does, however, find himself driven by passions and bound by ignorance and custom. Therefore he is actually not living according to the Logos. The facts of his daily life contradict his true nature. The Stoic message, then, is an appeal to abandon such a life, to live reasonably, to live according to the Logos, the Law of the universe. Such a "conversion" is really a decision to live according to this Law built into every man. Conversion to Stoicism is thus a decision to live according to one's true nature.

By the time of Paul, these basic beliefs had become commonplace because the wandering Stoic preachers exhorted slaves, merchants, housewives, students — anybody who would listen. The message was always the same: "Stop living such a foolish, hectic life in which you follow your emotion and ignorance. Discipline yourself. Give up the life of softness and pleasure-seeking. Do your duty as a man, wherever it may take you. Be ruled by reason. Be free to accept your destiny. Die manfully." The goal of Stoic life was a state of self-control and resistance to emotions, despite sickness, disaster, fear, or pain. Because the whole universe was believed to operate by law, it was considered that nothing could be changed anyway. For many, therefore, the Stoic position brought more resignation than positive self-control.

Today, many Christians are really Stoics whose chief teacher is Jesus. That is, they assume that the gospel is basically a summons to get into step with the universe on the basis of Jesus' teachings. To be sure, the value and insight of the Stoic gospel cannot be denied. Still, we must remember that mankind had such a gospel long before Jesus arrived on the scene — a gospel with no place for forgiveness.

2. Another religious option available was the exact opposite of Stoicism. This was Gnosticism (from the Greek word "gnosis" meaning knowledge. An "agnostic" is one who does *not* know; a Gnostic claims he *does*). It is helpful to see the major elements of the Gnostic understanding of man, even though the picture is put together from a variety of Gnostic sources. The Gnostics did not want to get into step with the universe but wanted to get out of it altogether. The fact that they were under the law of the universe did not make them rejoice but rather made them lament, because to them all man's problems come from having to live in this world. They believed their bodies were housing immortal, eternal souls, which were sparks of the divine, or splinters of the deity. They therefore regarded the body as the tomb of the soul, asserting that this immortal soul is away from home, living in a strange land (the body made of matter). Worst of all, they believed the soul does not even recognize its estrangement. But the Gnostics know it. They do not tell everybody, however, because not everybody has a soul capable of understanding; only those with divine sparks are capable of receiving true knowledge of man's state of affairs. The Gnostic considers himself a

member of the elite because his gospel provides this knowledge.

This knowledge centers in information about the soul, its origin and destiny — that is, what the soul is, where it came from, why it is here, where it shall go at death, and how it shall get there. The Gnostic claims he has saving knowledge because he believes that a divine savior descended from heaven to earth to bring it to him. After sojourning here briefly, the savior ascended to heaven again, according to Gnostic doctrine, making it possible for Gnostic souls to ascend too. The secret knowledge the savior brought not only informs the soul about its nature and destiny but helps it to escape the world at death. The Gnostics regarded the world as surrounded by planets (the way we regard the sun as circled by planets) which were really spheres of influence. In these heavenly bodies were thought to live enemy powers, hostile to the human soul. The universe thus was regarded as like a prison system with concentric rings of barbed wire, from which the soul can escape only if it has the proper passwords, secret information which the guards recognize. With this knowledge, the soul will be able to pass through these spheres and return to God. The Gnostic believes that the savior brings him this knowledge.

There has been a good deal of discussion among scholars concerning Gnosticism, especially since Gnostic gospels were found in Egypt in 1947.[3] It used to be thought that Gnosticism was a Christian heresy which arose after the New Testament period. But it is more and more clear that Gnosticism was also a religious movement which existed outside of Christianity and which began to influence it virtually from the time the first congregation was formed in Antioch. The scholars' debate concerns the nature and extent of this influence. Eventually, Christian Gnosticism became a mixture of Christianity and ancient mythology and philosophy, a sort of "theosophy." The second century saw the decisive battles with

Gnosticism, but the newly-found materials show that in many cases the line was hard to draw between a Gnostic Christian (or Christian Gnostic?) and an orthodox believer. Therefore the battle over Gnosticism was intense and prolonged. It was very much like a battle in modern times over whether one may regard Christian Science as a legitimate Christian "denomination" or not.

The irony is that, after the church fought so hard and seemingly won, Gnosticism was in many ways victorious. Not only did the church begin using the very language the Gnostics had once used (though in a somewhat different sense),[4] but many people to this day think that salvation consists of doing something to this invisible soul, that splinter of God that they believe is deposited behind the breastbones of mankind. Such an idea would have made Paul shudder.

3. There is still a third type of religious movement we must mention, the Mystery religions. There were many Mystery religions available, and they reached their zenith after the time of Paul. The Mysteries claimed that if one experienced a secret religious ritual (the mystery), he would be saved, because in the ritual he would be made a participant in eternal life. The priest of the Mystery religion promised that anyone who was initiated would be born again. (Thus Christians were not the only ones, and perhaps not the first, to use such language.) He would be made a partaker of a new quality of life, a divine life, because the ritual had the power to give it to him. The Mystery religion offered salvation by sacraments.[5]

Thus, the three "gospels" offered salvation in three different ways. The Stoics said salvation could be obtained by getting into step with the universe and its Law. This was a "do-it-yourself" salvation. The Gnostics and the Mystery priests said, "You can't do it by yourself," and provided help from the outside. The Gnostic offered saving knowledge, and the Mystery priest offered saving sacraments.

It is important to see that each of these three ways of salvation was grounded in its own way of looking at man and his situation in the world. Each kind of salvation was an answer to a particular problem; each salvation solved man's problem differently. The Stoic said man's problem was that he was contradicting his true nature; therefore the Stoic answer is to get in harmony with one's true nature and the universe by living by reason and discipline. The Gnostic said man's problem was that his body was in harmony with the world but that his soul was a prisoner of that body and did not know it; therefore the Gnostic answer was to provide the soul with the knowledge it needs to escape the body and the world altogether. The Mystery priest said man's problem was that his soul was simply inferior to that of the gods and no amount of information would help; therefore the Mystery answer was that the soul must partake of a higher grade of existence.[6]

We might also mention the Epicureans (who were also on Mars Hill) because they provided a secular alternative to all religions. They did not deny that the gods existed, but they did deny that the gods were concerned with men. The Epicureans also rejected any idea of life beyond death; hence they set themselves the task of finding a kind of life which provided the most satisfaction here and now. Epicurus, the founder, lived simply and serenely; for him "satisfaction" (or pleasure) included meditation and inner serenity. His teachings, however degenerated into that slogan known already to Paul, "Let us eat and drink, for tomorrow we die" (1 Corinthians 15:32). To a greater degree than many devout Christians realize, the Epicurean outlook (both in its purer and in its degenerate forms) expresses the mood of people today.

It was into such a world that Paul took the gospel about Jesus. How could he present it so that they understood what he was talking about and could accept it without confusing it with what they already had? With such questions in mind, we are prepared to climb Mars Hill and hear Paul. As we do, we realize that we face precisely the same sort of problems today.

ON MARS HILL

Today, Mars Hill is a scholars' no-man's land. It has been seared by crossfire for decades. Few passages in Acts have been more controversial than Acts 17, and virtually every interpretation is disputed by someone. There are two main controversies. One concerns the speech itself and its relation to Stoic ideas. The issue is whether the speech is so full of Stoic theology as to be an alien in the Bible, or whether it simply uses Stoic terms to talk about the biblical God. The second controversy concerns the speaker: Is it possible that Paul could have made such an address? Here we face the tension between Romans 1 and Acts 17. In Romans Paul has a gloomier outlook on paganism than is reflected here. In the main, German scholars doubt that Paul thought of paganism in the way which Acts reports, while English-speaking scholars think he did.

Both sides have oversimplified the second question. In Romans 1, addressed to Christians, Paul analyzed the situation of man in light of the law of God: Here paganism (and pagan religion) is regarded not as ignorance but as rejection of the truth of God. When Paul actually addressed pagans, however, in order to elicit their faith, it is possible that he used a different approach — not condemning their religion, but speaking as Acts reports. It is possible, of course, that Luke has inaccurately represented the nature of Paul's preaching. What needs to be remembered, though, is that Luke presents Paul in a way he regards to be relevant for his own time. Therefore the emphasis in the speech reflects Luke's understanding of the sort of thing Paul said. Actually, we have little evidence outside of Acts for knowing what Paul said *to* pagans when he presented the gospel to them; Romans simply shows us what he said to Christians *about* the pagans.

In any case, for our purpose, these controversies are not crucial. We are interested in what the text of Acts means.

We begin by seeing the story as a whole (17:16-34). We observe that Paul is in a different kind of situation on Mars Hill from that of the synagogue in Athens where he also preached. In the synagogue, he preached to a congregation assembled for worship. There Paul was at home. Both he and his hearers believed that the Bible was the Word of God; therefore, an argument from Scripture had weight if it could be shown to be a valid interpretation. Moreover, in the synagogue Paul could assume a common body of beliefs about the world, Israel, the Messiah, and the coming judgment. True, Judaism had wide latitude of belief about messiahship, but everyone at least knew what was being discussed and shared a common point of departure. In short, in the synagogue Paul was a Jew among Jews, and was proclaiming the meaning of their existence as illumined by the messiahship of Jesus. In other words, for Paul this synagogue-situation was a kind of "Christendom," a context in which the setting was congenial to his message about the Messiah.

But on the streets of Athens and on Mars Hill *none* of these things could be assumed. Here was an entirely different situation. To quote Scripture, to talk about the meaning of Israel's history and Israel's hope would only have been a waste of time. The hearers might agree that Jesus' life corresponded to certain elements in the Jewish Bible and still say, "So what? So some Jews think their sacred writings come true in another Jew — just what does that mean to me, a Greek in Athens, a good Stoic?" Luke hints that Paul tried such an approach. Paul probably dressed up his synagogue preaching in Greek clothes (as we might say, he "made it interesting") and talked about Jesus and resurrection. But he failed completely to be even understood, let alone believed, because they thought he was talking about two new gods, Jesus and Resurrection.[r] In a book like Acts, which emphasizes the success of early Christian preaching, this first experience in Athens stands out as a total failure — a failure caused by the fact that there was not enough common ground between Paul and his hearers for them to understand. This story is a classic example of a preacher saying one thing and the people hearing another.

But Paul had another opportunity, and this time he tried to find common ground, a point of contact. This is the famous speech found in verses 22-31, in which he was able to carry the audience along for most of the way. This sermon was not a total failure, because a few did believe, a small nucleus of a church. But still, it was not the kind of success story *Reader's Digest* loves to print. Why, then, did Luke bother to tell it at all? Because he saw it as a symbol of Christian preaching in the Greek world. The story shows what it means to witness to the resurrection in a world without Christendom.

Our next task, then, is to look at the sermon itself. We begin with the core, verses 24-29. This concerns the Creator and his creation. It is not a lecture on the nature and existence of God but an exposition of the relation between God the Creator and man the created. We may list the main ideas of the sermon-heart quickly: (1) God created the world and is not a part of it, nor does he depend on it in any way. In fact, the meaning of creation is precisely the opposite — everything depends on God, who is to be distinguished from what he has made. (2) The Creator determines the destinies of men and nations. Here is a way of saying that God is the shaper of human affairs, whether men know this fact or not, whether they acknowledge it or not. The sermon declares the guiding work of God to be a fact of human life. (3) God wills men to seek him so that they may reach him. The seeking, however, is not a searching for an absent deity but a recognizing of total dependence on the God who is at hand. The quotations from the pagan poets emphasize the kinship between God and man. In the setting of this sermon, however, they also point to the dependence of man on God, for being an offspring means being a dependent. Having our existence modified by God at every hand (as we live, move, and have our being in him) means that we have no independence at all which is not conferred by this God. (4) Consequently, God is not like things men make, but is like man himself. The things men make tell us about men, but they cannot tell us about God. Man himself is the witness to God.

One of the reasons there has been so much discussion of this sermon, which we have analyzed in extremely brief fashion, is that everything in it can be traced in two directions. It has living relations on both sides of the family tree of ideas. It points, on the one hand, to the Old Testament belief about the Creator and man's history, followed by the theme of judgment (which appears in the framework of the speech). On the other hand, its words and phrases can also be traced to the religious philosophy of the time, Stoicism. This relationship is exactly what Luke intended to show. He shows how Paul made contact with his environment, with another faith, how he tried to elicit a conversation with his hearers. They might not agree with everything he said, but they understood what he was talking about this time. It is worth exploring the kind of contact Paul actually made here. For our purpose, we may restrict ourselves to the Stoic hearers.[8]

The Stoic was a thinker with wide horizons. For him, God was universal, and God was one; there could be only one God behind the many gods and religions. To the Stoic, all religions were simply different expressions of the same reality, local options of the same Law. Therefore when Paul said that God did not live in a particular shrine but transcended them all, the Stoic would nod in agreement. Moreover, the Stoic would accept Paul's talking about God as the lord of heaven and earth, because to the Stoic this would be simply an unsual way of saying that the universe was ruled by Law (to the Stoic, God and Law are almost the same thing). Besides, the Stoic would agree that all men are made of the same stuff (or from the same man),[9] though divided by race, history, and culture. One of the great Stoic doctrines was the equality of all men, slave or sovereign. For the Stoic, all men were equal because the same Logos was in them all. Furthermore, the Stoic would agree that God is not to be compared to any statue of him, but is really everywhere at hand. In other words, the Stoic could listen understandingly to this speech. He could hear what was being said, because Paul was dealing with questions about God and man, questions with which the Stoic had been grappling for years — on his own terms, in his own way.

But the Stoic would face new things here too. To begin, he would not be used to talking about God and the world in just these terms either. The Stoic tended to be a pantheist; that is, he tended so strongly to see God (the Law) in everything that everything was an expression or form of God's power and order. It was hard for him to see any difference between God and the world. Therefore he could not really conceive of any kind of God beyond the universe, any kind of deity who transcended the cosmos. The word "cosmos" for him meant the totality of what is, just as our word "space" refers not simply to our universe, but to the totality of universes, including those not seen yet. It is just as hard for us to think of anything "beyond space" as it was for the Stoic to think of a deity beyond the cosmos. Yet Paul spoke about God and the world in a way that implied that God was really distinct from it. In other words, this sermon met and challenged the Stoic in a way that could get a hearing and a response, a genuine discussion of how God and the world are related.

In the same way, Paul took up the idea that every man is religious by saying that God has created all nations to dwell on earth and to seek God. But Paul expressed some doubt whether these religious quests are successful (this questioning is clearer in the Greek text than in our translations). Paul shares the Stoic belief that all men seek God, but he raises a question as to whether they reach him. This doubt is all the more intriguing in light of the next statement that God is so near that we live and move and exist in him. The Stoic would prefer to put this relationship the other way around, that God (the Law or Logos) lives in us, but he would not quibble.

The real point of discussion is whether this nearness of God to man means that all quests for God are inevitably successful, whether all religions lead to the same true God inevitably. Paul implies that they do not, for, while he admits the fact that the search is universal, he denies that all religions are more or less different forms of the same thing, the way chihuahuas, boxers, and collies are all dogs. For Paul, the fact that there is one God and that all men are religious does not mean that all religions are equally valid. Indeed, for him some are in error and others are in ignorance. Ignorance is what he emphasizes here. Nevertheless, the oneness of God does mean to him that there is only one God actually being worshiped, whether correctly or not. This is why Paul does not damn the religions of Athens but admits that they are quests for the only God there is — quests without understanding, quests derailed by idolatries of every kind, but nonetheless real quests for the real God. Here again, Paul accepts the seeking without taking the solution, and thereby he opens another opportunity to present the gospel in terms which the hearer could grasp.

Now we may turn to the framework into which these ideas are set (verses 22-23, 30-31). The first part announces Paul's intent to deal with the unperceptive worship in Athens, and the second calls for a decision as a result of his critique. It is the second that concerns us now — the summons to repent.

The sermon says that God has tolerated this situation of worship without understanding, but that he now commands repentance.[10] What does it mean for men *on Mars Hill* to repent? Literally, the word translated "repent" (*metanoein*) means "to change one's mind." But the New Testament writers were steeped in the Greek translation of the Old Testament, made several centuries earlier in Egypt. Therefore if we want to know what they meant by this word, we must note not only what the Greek word ordinarily meant but especially what it meant in their Greek Bible. Here we find that *metanoein* translated a Hebrew verb *shubh* which means "to turn," "to turn back." Primary emphasis is not on a change of thinking, but on one of direction; on a change of action, not simply one of ideas. In the Hebrew Bible the call to repentance is almost always a call to turn back to God, to make a U-turn. This is exactly what Jesus summoned his hearers to do — believe his message that God's kingdom was at hand and turn back to God as a response to this nearness (Mark 1:14f.). He did not ask them to repent so that they would be ready in case God should come, but because God has already seized the initiative. God's coming in kingly power was both judgment and forgiveness at the same time.

Here in Acts 17, however, the word has a somewhat different meaning because the situation in which it is used has changed. It is no longer Israel that is addressed, but Gentile Stoics. *Here* the word means a summons to turn away from the old unknowing, unperceptive worship of God and toward the true God, the Creator in whom all men live. In other words, *here* repentance means dealing decisively with this ignorance of the true God and acting to express this new understanding. Here repentance means admitting the failure of past worship and turning toward a new worship of God with proper understanding of who God is, and what man is. It is important to see that here, as in the synagogue, Paul speaks in the same category, "Repent." Yet the demand is not identical, for the content has been expanded. Repentance for the Jew means turning away from the rejection of Jesus and toward the Messiah Jesus. Repentance for the Stoic, however, means turning away from his understanding of God as the built-in Law of the universe (actually his ignorance of God) to worship the God who transcends creation. In other words, in this sermon on Mars Hill, Paul recognizes that each person must make his own repentance in his own way, in light of the situation in which the gospel finds him. This point is absolutely essential for any effort to present the gospel in a world without Christendom.

There is another thing we must see in the framework of the sermon. Paul gives the whole appeal a sense of urgency by referring to the coming judgment. In so doing he alludes to the heart of the Christian gospel, the decisive significance of Jesus for every man, a significance attested by the resurrection (as discussed in Chapter 3). Note that here Paul does not even name Jesus, but simply refers to his role. Note also that here Paul reached the limits of his sermon. He got no farther, because resurrection was one thing no one wanted to hear about, especially if it included being judged by a resurrected person. Later, Paul wrote the Corinthians that the gospel was foolishness to the Greeks, and this reaction is precisely what we observe on Mars Hill.[11]

The Stoics did not want to hear about resurrection and judgment, because this doctrine simply was unnecessary in their smoothly-working universe where Providence determined everything anyway. They believed that there would be a general burning up of the world some day, but this was simply a necessary step before the whole cycle began over again. There were many such cycles in the life of the universe, they thought, but no such thing as final judgment. Paul's idea was therefore sheer nonsense to the Stoics. The Gnostics did not want to hear about resurrection either, because for them the problem of man could be solved only by release from the body altogether and not by having it resurrected in some transformed state. Moreover, the Gnostic saw no point in being judged for what one did in the body. The Mystery priest likewise saw no meaning in resurrection, because he believed he had already been transformed into a half-god. Some of the Mystery religions celebrated myths of gods who died and came to life; however, these experiences in the god's life did not qualify him to judge man but to transform him into an immortal being. Because the Epicureans denied all life after death, Paul's words seemed to them scarcely worth taking seriously.

When Paul brought up the subject of resurrection and judgment, then, there was no discussion, because this topic was not something they considered seriously enough to discuss. They either snickered or begged off until another day. And so the story ends. Luke shows that there comes a time when the witness to the resurrection can do no more than state his position, share his insights, and leave the rest to God. In fact, the story suggests that reaching such a point is a necessary part of communication. As my colleague, Professor Sellers has written, "The point of contact is always a 'point of conflict'. . . ."[12]

THE STRATEGY OF WITNESS

What does this glimpse of Paul on Mars Hill suggest for our witness in our own pluralistic setting? Among the many things we may learn on this hill, the following are especially important.

This account reminds us that communication is not simply broadcasting. In broadcasting, one turns on his transmitter and begins to speak. But communication is related to communion, to a meeting of persons. Acts 17 is important because it shows us that Paul could go a long way to meet the minds of his hearers. He himself insists that on one occasion he is a Jew, on another occasion a Gentile (1 Corinthians 9:19-23). Is this the admission of an unscrupulous propagandist who will say whatever he thinks his audience wants to hear? There is no doubt that Paul was accused of this kind of vacillation.

For Paul, however, this strategy was part of the freedom of the gospel. In his view, gospel freedom brought not only liberty to the soul but freedom for strategy, freedom in ways of presenting the good news to others. Now, as then, this free-dom is essential for genuine communication of the gospel. Just as there was no communication in Athens so long as Paul simply preached synagogue sermons to Gentiles, so there is no communication of the gospel so long as we simply aim the traditional gospel barrage of Christendom at the public.

Meeting another person with gospel-given freedom means recognizing first of all that this man *has some kind* of faith. It may be faith in something that turns out to be no God at all, an idol of some kind; it may also be faith in no faith — that is, he may have faith that man can get along without God alto-gether. Therefore, a genuine meeting between myself and another man can take place only when I recognize that he is a believer of some sort, a man who is trying to cope with the problems of life on the basis of some kind of faith, some kind of commitment to what he cannot prove. I may be convinced that *my* faith compass is the only one that points to true north; still, I am under obligation to look at *his* and to under-stand how he uses it to find his way, because he is no less than a man and I am no more than one. In other words, to com-municate with him means to recognize that, despite whatever faith (religious or non-religious) separates me from another believer, he and I stand on common ground for two reasons: (a) Since God made us both, we both live on the same side of the line between God and man; (b) God sent his Son across that line for both of us. This other person is my *fellow-man* before he is either my adversary or object of evangelism.[18] Therefore I must be willing to listen to him, and to listen with him for the Word of God. Then, and perhaps only then, is it possible for me to bear a witness to the gospel that will really be heard. Freedom for communication in communion is a freedom based on a full acceptance of the fact that the Chris-tian is a creature pointing fellow creatures to God, sharing with his fellow men the good news about what God has done. This is not freedom to prove his religion is superior to theirs.

It is important to remember also that this freedom is not simply a subtle strategy to maneuver people into "accepting Christ." Much modern evangelism is nothing more than manipulation of persons in the name of God. Here again, Paul is wiser. Paul can be a Jew or a Greek as the occasion requires. He recognizes that there is no particular set of words, no set of cultural norms and ideas so sacred it must be used at all times. Just as there is no messianic culture (Chapter 4, pages 95-102), so there is no messianic form for the gospel. The gospel is not a relic of sacred words and phrases to be passed on with veneration, but a living message about a reality that transcends all vocabularies and methods. Paul is therefore free to enter into conversation, into communication with Pharisee and pagan alike because he knows that neither religion is absolute, yet both are grappling with the enigmas of human life. Both are clarified and, where necessary, corrected by the meaning of Jesus as good news. Paul's task is to make this good news apparent. Paul knows that, since men are saved by God's grace and not by the words they use to say so, he can be free to range over the whole sweep of his own culture to find words and ideas to apprehend men wherever they are, and to tell them the good news right there. He does not think it necessary to enroll the Stoics in a sidewalk seminar in biblical theology first.

Moreover, because Paul regards all men as sinners equally (though not identically) in need of grace regardless of the culture in which they sin or the vocabulary they may use, he knows there is no pure language for the gospel. He does not speak angelic language made in heaven, but human words used to bear divine wisdom — clay pots with treasures, he calls them (2 Corinthians 4:7). He alerts his readers to beware of those who present themselves on any other basis. Paul does not arrive in Athens as an angel from heaven with a virgin-pure theological vocabulary, but as a dusty sinner-saint with a prison record for witnessing to the resurrection, Jesus' and his own (Rom. 6:1-11; Col. 2:12f.). Paul reminds us that the church does not need salesmen of salvation, but serious witnesses to the gospel who are willing to risk meeting another human being wherever he may be, in whatever culture he may find himself, because God undertook just this kind of encounter when he sent his Son into human affairs. And there, on the borderline of their common situation as sons of Adam, the witnessing to the resurrection takes place in freedom and in power when the Christian can testify that he is a son of the New Adam also.

Paul on Mars Hill also teaches us that freedom for such communication is possible only when we are willing to risk failure. Even Paul's second attempt was not a glowing success. At the same time the story permits us to see that the faith of Dionysius and others had integrity, as shown by the fact that they were free to hear and reject this news about Jesus.

What is a valid decision for Christ? Only the decider and God can know. But, still, it is legitimate for others to say that no commitment is worth much unless the person's faith is a deliberate choice, a risk, a wager, an act whereby he puts his life and destiny into the hands of the kind of God revealed in the story of Jesus. When the gospel is presented in a way that the depth of the decision is clear, more people may respond with "No, thank you" than "Amen." Real communication of the gospel in a pluralistic world does not take place until this risk is accepted, until the man of another faith is granted the freedom to make a real choice, Yes or No. Wherever the gospel is presented in such a way that only a fool would turn it down, it is betrayed by its most ardent friends.

Paul accepted the risk of failure on Mars Hill. When his hearers began to see the line between their faith and his, and sensed what was involved in believing what he had to say, they said they had heard enough. Acts shows that there was a difference in the way they rejected Paul's message before and after the Mars Hill episode. The first time they did not know what they were turning down. Paul's speech, in this light, was his effort to make sure that they got the point clearly enough that their response would have integrity. His strategy was to present the gospel in such a way that they could make a significant choice, one that involved real issues and not phony ones. This kind of strategy calls for a concentration of energy and imagination far beyond what is usually expended in revival meetings, and in many other evangelistic endeavors. It calls for a personal meeting of man with man, faith with faith.

The church in America lives with confused images of its work. It admires the good shepherd who goes after that one sheep, but often it actually operates like a cowboy. That is, the church is not really prepared to risk seeking that single sheep so that he may be rescued where he is, because it is more interested in the annual round-up at revival time when the half-churched can be enrolled again. While we are fixing the corral, perhaps we ought to pause long enough to ponder the meaning of Mars Hill.

WHAT BELONGS TO CAESAR

Be subject for the Lord's sake . . . to the emperor as supreme or to governors as sent by him. . . . Live as free men, yet without using your freedom as a pretext for evil. . . . Fear God. Honor the emperor.

—1 PETER (2:13-17)

My relation to him [the emperor] is one of freedom; for I have but one true Lord, the God omnipotent and eternal.

—TERTULLIAN, A.D. 200

*There is no State, nor is there any nation, to which the text applies that Christ is with them until the end of the world. For this reason, there are no politics, not even Church politics, that do not come under the Scriptural sentence, "All flesh is as grass." ***

—HANS ASMUSSEN, a Christian in Germany, 1934

*The supreme Magistracie of this Kingdome we believe to be the King and Parliament freely chosen . . . and that in all those civill Lawes . . . we are bound to yeeld subjection . . . in the Lord. . . . But if God with-hold the Magistrates allowance [tolerance] . . . yet we must not withstanding proceed together in Christian communion, not daring to give place to suspend our practice, but to walk in obedience to Christ . . . even in the midst of all trialls and afflictions. . . . And if any take this that we have said, to be heresie, then doe wee with the Apostle freely confesse, that after the way which they call heresie, worship we the God of our Fathers. . . . ****

—LONDON CONFESSION OF BAPTISTS, 1644

TEXT OF ACTS: 16:16-40; 17:1-9; 19:23-41; 21:17-22:30

THINGS TO LOOK FOR:

1. Since the problem of the Christian and the state looms so large in the latter part of Acts, it will be necessary to survey material on this subject as a whole, especially from 16:16 onward.

2. The story of Paul in Philippi (16:11-40) is best known for the report of the earthquake and the jailer's conversion. Note the charge against Paul. What does Luke want the reader to understand about the Christian's relation to the government?

3. Paul's stay in Thessalonica is told briefly (17:1-9). Note the charge against Paul here. What does this accusation reveal about the way he presented Jesus as the Christ?

4. The riot at Ephesus is told in some detail (19:23-41). Note carefully the issue that triggered the riot. What does Luke want the reader to understand about Christianity's place in society and its relation to the state?

5. Paul's appearance in Jerusalem caused a riot reported in 21:17ff. The Assassins mentioned in verse 38 were a revolutionary group of patriots, the Zealots (see p. 86). Why does Luke consider this detail worth reporting?

6. The scene reported in Chapter 26 (building on the preparation in Chapter 25) reaches a climax at 26:30-32. Notice how the emphasis on Paul's innocence echoes the same emphasis in Luke's report about Jesus' trial: Luke 23:1-5, 13-25. Why does Luke bear down on this point?

7. Luke's attitude toward the state should be compared with that of Paul and the writer of Revelation. What is the main point Paul makes in Romans 13:1-7? Why does he encourage the Roman readers to be loyal citizens? What are the chief dangers in the interpretation of this passage?

8. Revelation 13 reports a vision of a strange beast from the sea (the symbolic source of evil). The beast represents Rome. Notice that this is worshiped and that it harms the saints. Observe also that the other beast (verse 11 ff.) is an agent for the first. The second beast is usually regarded as the emperor Domitian, who reigned near the end of the first century. Because the writer regarded the time of Domitian as the time of Nero (the first persecutor of the church) all over again, he gave Domitian (the second beast) the number 666, the symbol for Nero.[1] Contrast the attitude toward the Roman empire in Romans 13 with that in Revelation. To which of these is Luke closer?

CHAPTER SIX

WHAT BELONGS TO CAESAR

THE SUPREME COURT IS MORE CONCERNED WITH THE ISSUES OF church and state than ever before, and the end is not in sight.[2] The growing number of cases before the court is a symptom of the fact that Protestant Christianity is not the only voice being heard. The Catholic, the Jew, the Mormon, the secularist — each is insisting that this is his country too, and that he must not be treated as if he were simply a permanent guest in a Protestant house. The more these and other non-Protestant groups demand freedom from being coerced into conforming to the Protestant idea of what American society should be like, the clearer it is that Protestant Christendom has eroded away. This is what living in a democratic society has come to mean.

Unfortunately, Protestant Christianity came to think of itself as the spiritual bulwark of the American Way of Life, when it was merely the buttress for the old status quo. This self-understanding has made it difficult for Protestantism to accept changes. Such inner resistance to change has received significant support from the world situation. In our time, when the world is curtained by iron, bamboo, and sugar cane, some Americans suspect that every demand for change is a devious communist conspiracy.

But the facts do not justify this combination of fear and fervor. When zealous preachers make Protestant Christianity the religious foundation of the American Way of Life, they have in mind some scrubbed and polished picture of America as a land of God-fearing farmers and small-town merchants who take part in civic affairs without "dirty politics" and who stream into white churches whose slender spires pierce the trees. This is the America of *Our Town* and the *Reader's Digest*. This is the America which exists only in our ideology, in the propaganda we aim at ourselves. But the actual American Way was never so romantic as this lovely picture; instead, it is based on exploitation of minorities more than on equity; its law is more the law of the jungle than the law of God; the sign in which we conquer the world is not the sign of the cross but of the dollar. We come close to recognizing the real American Way of Life when we note that in this country everything is for sale — every article has a price, every allegiance can be bought (or bartered for influence or prestige), every virtue can be priced. These seamy elements of our society counterweight the romantic pictures we hold before our eyes. These are not the only elements, but they are there and have been there from the beginning. The church can no longer ignore these facts. The demands of minority groups for full equality now make this situation unmistakably clear. When the church makes itself the guarantor of this American Way, it blesses the bad with the good, the crass commercialism of the hucksters with the voluntary civic-mindedness of the United Givers Fund. The reason is that the church commonly fails to distinguish between the ideals praised on July 4 and the actual American Way of Life as it is lived on April 15.

Moreover, in our cold war situation, there are many subtle pressures in the land to keep us from seeing the truth about ourselves. People who trumpet their patriotism reveal how fragile their faith in America is by their nervousness when anyone speaks critically of it. Actually, the one who is unafraid to give or receive criticisms, including basic ones, is the person whose loyalty has the deeper roots. Our present situation tempts Christians into precarious kinds of patriotism. In the determination to stop communism, many people have come to regard patriotism as a religious posture, and religious convictions have become marks of patriotism. This confusion is expressed in the fact that communists must be referred to as "atheistic"; those who oppose them are therefore automatically regarded as religious. In our time, pietism and patriotism have entered a common-law marriage, and the issue of such union is rapidly becoming apparent. For one thing, the things that belong to God now belong to Caesar too.

The posture of the church in the United States is made all the more precarious when we see it in global perspective. Half a century of revolutions has brought about a resurgence of nationalism in every country, whether it be the aggressive nationalism of a Nazi Germany, of an Islamic Egypt, of a Marxist Russia, or of a post-Protestant America. The church today exists in a world divided by sensitive nationalisms.[8] Wherever the church is found, Christians consider themselves good citizens, though each group defines "good citizenship" differently. But this assortment of loyalties is precisely what creates the problem, for if Christians everywhere were to identify themselves as closely with the flag that flies over them as some have in this country, then the universal church would be simply a religious replica of the divided world and would have no alternative to offer at all. Yet the church is not simply the religious counterpart of the world's political divisions.

The criticisms aimed at the admission of the Russian Orthodox Church into the World Council of Churches illustrate this dilemma clearly. Americans become alarmed and suspicious whenever they hear that the Moscow patriarch champions "peace" and speaks well of the new Soviet way of life; yet they think it perfectly natural and desirable that American pulpits should ring with the gospel of free enterprise as the divinely-willed economic system of the kingdom of God. In such a situation the time is ripe to discern what really does belong to God and what belongs to Caesar.

This matter is far too complex to be settled decisively in a few pages. Looking at Acts, however, can help us by showing us the nature of the problem, and the direction in which the answer may lie.

GOD AND CAESAR, THEN AND NOW

First, we must see that this incestuous relation between church and state, faith and patriotism, is not a modern problem at all. In fact, it is not even a peculiarly Christian one. Looking at Acts in proper perspective means that we must see it in light of the biblical and pagan backgrounds of the matter.

The biblical background of the problem begins with the Old Testament, especially in the time of King David (around 1000 B.C.). During the time of the monarchy (from shortly before David's time to 586 B.C., when the Babylonians sacked Jerusalem the second time) there was no problem of "church and state," because the religious community and the political community were identical. To put the situation into modern terms, Israel was a sort of Hebrew "Christendom." The head of state, the king, was not merely a secular ruler of a secular government; he reigned in the name of God. The situation was somewhat similar to that in Puritan-controlled New England. The prophets regarded this arrangement as ideal — at that time. But when the nation was destroyed, the situation changed. Except for a few years during the Maccabean period (165 B.C. to 63 B.C.) when the king made himself high priest as well, such an integration of church and state ceased in Israel. Even today, modern Israel is a secular state, separate from the religious community. The youth regard themselves as Israelis, some of whom are Jews — that is, they are citizens of Israel, and some practice the Jewish religion. Such a situation is not only a painful disappointment to many orthodox rabbis in the Israel of today, but would have been unheard of in the time of David.

After the Jewish people became subject to foreign rule, however, the problem of "church and state" emerged, though during the period when Judea was part of the Persian empire the issue was not clear. But in the fourth century B.C., Alexander's Greek armies swept across the world and brought with them the Greek style of life in much the same way that the American G.I. Americanized half the globe during World War II. Thereafter, the Jews of Palestine (and elsewhere) had to choose whether to be faithful to the old customs of Judaism, or to adopt Greek ways, or to find some way to have both. All three attempts were made.

At first the Greek rulers who succeeded Alexander were neutral in these matters. But, in the second century B.C., Palestine became a part of the territory ruled by Antiochus Epiphanes. Perceiving that much of the Jewish resistance to his administration stemmed from allegiance to Jewish religious practices and beliefs, he brought military and police power to force the Jews to abandon their religion and their customs. Here the tension between "church and state" burst into flames, and Jews have known its burning ever since.

When Antiochus Epiphanes forbade circumcision and Sabbath observance, he galvanized the Jews into revolution. The Book of Daniel, written at this time, reflects the bitterness clearly. This crisis produced not only a theoretical issue of "church and state," but an intensely moral one as well — the problem of the martyr. Never before did the Old Testament writers have to face this question. Earlier, the authors of Deuteronomy and Proverbs had assured the believers that the faithful would prosper and the wicked would suffer, but now it was the faithful who were suffering and the wicked were oppressing them. Worst of all, some Jews were collaborating with the evil oppressors. Here was the struggle for religious freedom, and its outlines were etched in blood.

The Christian church was born before this problem had been solved. True, in these matters the Romans were much more tolerant than Antiochus Epiphanes had been. Nonetheless, the problem was keen: What shall be the attitude of a devout Jew toward the Roman occupation army? Some, like the priestly Sadducees, believed that the only realistic thing to do was to collaborate, so that the temple services could continue in peace and security. Others, like the Pharisees, found it possible to concentrate on clearly religious duties under an occupation army and wait until God himself saw fit to change things. Others, the Zealots, were convinced that the only faithful policy was opposition and subversion, even if it meant murder and revolution. The church was born in a land seething with revolt, in which political issues were the occasions for fierce loyalties and bitter controversies. We must picture the Palestine of Jesus as being like East Germany or Formosa, in which the native population as a whole has been controlled by foreign military occupation on the one hand, and split into rival factions contending for the right to manipulate the situation on the other.

The New Testament does not have a single attitude toward the state, but rather a double one. The twin points of view are symbolized by Romans 13 and Revelation 13, neither of which was written in Palestine, but both of which reflect the situation of a church whose roots were in the Palestinian situation. According to Revelation 13, the Roman empire is a devilish beast which makes war on the saints and is worshiped by the pagans. This worship is instigated by the imperial priesthood or the emperor himself. There is much that is obscure in this chapter, but there is no doubt about the main point — that the Roman state is depicted as the power of Satan who is ravaging the church. This attitude reflects the experience of the church at the end of the first century. On the other hand, Romans 13 was written a generation earlier, before the Roman government had yet lifted a finger against the Christians. Hence Paul is much more optimistic about the place of the state: It is God's servant for good. The innocent man has therefore no need to fear the state; to the contrary, Paul believes, the Christian is to support it with taxes and allegiance.

In other words, the difference between Romans and Revelation is not simply the result of two writers having different theologies; it results from the shift of the situation of the church. In the time of Paul, no Christian had yet been martyred by the state; but, by the time of Revelation, the church (in Rome at least) had seen its brothers die through torture. After the great fire in Rome in A.D. 64, Nero made the Christians the scapegoats, and the young congregation was baptized in its own blood. Tradition says, Paul and Peter were both killed at this time. Thirty years later, when Revelation was written, the emperor Domitian was about to lay hands on the church again, and probably his local administrators in Asia Minor had already done so.

The situation of the church with regard to the state shifted back and forth between the two possibilities of coexistence (as represented in Romans) and persecution (as seen in Revelation). In A.D. 312, however, all this changed, for the emperor Constantine proclaimed toleration for the church. Within another hundred years, a successor proclaimed Christianity the official religion of the empire. It is still not clear whether the changes wrought by Constantine marked the triumph or the defeat of the gospel. In any case he made Christendom possible.[4]

Next, we must look at the problem from the pagan side. In the Roman empire the problems of church and state are really the issues of how the religions of personal salvation (discussed in Chapter 5) are related to the state religion.

There was a persistent tension between the official Roman religion and the "working" religions of the people. The purpose of the official religion of Rome was to provide precise religious ceremonies to the gods who guaranteed the stability and power of Rome. This is why the Roman Senate was deeply concerned lest this official religion be undermined in any way, for such action would weaken the state. On the other hand, the average man was more concerned for his soul than for the state, except in times of national emergency. Hence, he sought a religion which met his needs. At first, he turned to the ancient folk religions of Italy, but, by the time of the New Testament, he had become more interested in the religions of salvation from the Orient, especially the Mystery cults. The Roman Senate opposed such imported religions and at first forbade them altogether. But, one by one, they forced their way into Rome and came to be accepted by the Senate. The history of religion in Rome is really the history of the immigration of the gods and their naturalization as Roman deities. A bird's-eye view would show the coming of Christianity from Jerusalem as the arrival of just one more religion of salvation from the East. Hence, the same attitudes would apply to it as to the rest: suspicion, then suppression, finally acceptance. Professor Grant puts it this way:

> The Christians were thus punished because their religion was believed to be inimical to the interests of the state. This belief was shared by the people and the rulers alike, but only in times of crisis did it become a belief which required aggressive action. Ordinarily Christians were regarded as potentially but not actually dangerous to the peace and security of the Roman empire.[5]

In addition to this patriotic character of official religion, we must note another factor — the worship of the emperor. Shortly before the time of Christ, Caesar Augustus promoted the worship of the ancient Roman gods. Though he insisted that he was not divine, he permitted people in the eastern provinces to worship his "genius." The "genius" of the emperor was not simply his intellectual ability, but the divine power at work in and through him. In Egypt, where the kings had always been worshiped as gods, it was natural simply to say that the Roman emperor was divine. In other places where the kings had been believed to be the agents of the gods, the worship of the emperor's "genius" was welcomed with enthusiasm, because the theory behind the ritual meant that the emperor was on good terms with the gods, and that, in turn, the empire would be blessed with peace and prosperity. Therefore the reign of Augustus was marked by a flood of hymns and poems praising the emperor as the personal bringer of salvation for society.

Many important details of this emperor cult are no longer available to historians, but two things are clear enough. One is that the government regarded the worship of the emperor as an act of patriotism and not much more. It was encouraged because it promoted the unity and stability of the empire. The other thing that is clear is that the average person did not regard this as the religion for his soul any more than most Americans look on saluting the flag as a religious rite. (The Jehovah's Witness, however, does regard this salute as a form of worship. The situation of the Jehovah's Witness and his refusal to salute the flag is virtually the same as that of the early Christians and the imperial altars.[6])

Like the Jehovah's Witnesses today, the Christians and Jews then did not accept the government's interpretation of the matter. For them, there could be no religious ceremony in the name of any Caesar. The emperors used all sorts of divine titles for themselves, such as Savior, Lord, and God. The ordinary citizen saw no more offense in these labels than the average person today does in speaking of a minister as "a divine." But the Jew and the Christian saw in it nothing less than blasphemy. For the Christians and Jews, only God was divine; and, for the Christians, only Jesus was Lord.

When the Romans learned that the Christians were reluctant to "go along" and that some actually refused, they saw this reaction as nonviolent resistance to law and order, a threat to the security of the state, and a mark of disloyalty. The Roman attitude is like the earlier American attitude toward the Jehovah's Witnesses (though fortunately no martyrdom has been involved in the present-day parallel); hence, various measures were taken against the Christians from time to time. Some confessors of Lord Jesus were executed because they would not worship the genius of Lord Caesar; others were exiled. Many were begged to drop just a pinch of incense on the altar and say the simplest possible word of devotion, to meet "the letter of the law." The irony of this situation did not escape the Christian lawyer, Tertullian, who noted at the beginning of the third century that criminals were being tortured to make them confess, but Christians were confessing and being tortured to make them deny. Many did. Many refused as well.

Such is the kind of situation which was behind the book of Revelation. Acts was written only a few years earlier, and therefore it handles the problem in a way which spoke to the church as it faced the gathering storm. With this general situation in mind, we can now see what Luke has to say.

THE GOSPEL ON TRIAL

To get the full scope of Luke's approach, it is important to begin with Volume One, Luke's Gospel.

Luke puts the life of Jesus into a clearly political setting. For one thing, he reports that Jesus was born at that moment when the Jews were deeply humiliated by the census (Luke 2:1f.). The census was not simply a head count but actually a tax assessment. At times, such registrations provoked open violence, because they expressed too clearly the servile place of the people (as Acts 5:37 hints). At this low point in Israel's life, says Luke, the Messiah was born. But more important is the fact that Luke tells us precisely what Roman authorities were in power when Jesus began his mission (Luke 3:1). He provides this information partly because he wants to be a historian as well as an evangelist, and partly because he has a sense of the hidden tension between these two rulers, Lord Jesus and Lord Caesar.

Still more significant for recognizing our problem is the way Luke tries to shift the blame for Jesus' death to the Jews. All the gospels have this tendency, but it is particularly clear in Luke. Three times, he says, Pilate found Jesus "not guilty" of revolutionary activity and tried to release him (23:4f., 13-16, 22-25). Luke wanted his readers to have no doubt: Jesus was innocent of political insurrection. Luke was not afraid to describe Jesus as Son of David and King of Israel, but for Luke these terms referred to spiritual and moral leadership, not national rule. By making clear that the resurrected Jesus would not even discuss the restoration of the kingdom to Israel (Acts 1:6f.), Luke insisted that the movement which came from Jesus was not a kind of Christian Zionism.

Volume One gives us still another hint of Luke's ideas of church and state. In Luke 21 he has reworked Mark 13, a collection of prophecies about the final catastrophe of history. Here Luke reports Jesus' words about the coming persecution of the church: "This will be a time for you to bear testimony," that is, for witness. This will be an effective witness: "I will give you a mouth and wisdom which none of your adversaries will be able to withstand or contradict" (Luke 21:10-15). Hence, we may expect Acts to show the Christians engaged in the fulfillment of these words of Jesus; we are not disappointed. The commission to bear witness (with which Acts begins in 1:6-8) is preceded (in Luke's Gospel) by the promise that this witness shall be given partly in court. In Acts, therefore, the gospel is on trial.

We may begin by noting how the first major unit of Acts ends: "So the church throughout all Judea and Galilee and Samaria had peace and was built up; and walking in the fear of the Lord and in the comfort of the Holy Spirit it was multiplied" (9:31). To appreciate this statement, we must bear in mind that the story of the church up to this point is one in which the believers had been in some kind of trouble with civil authorities virtually ever since Pentecost. This summary is really a sigh of relief for a moment of peace.

But this peace was only an interlude. In A.D. 42, one of the twelve apostles was executed (Acts 12:1f.). Twenty years later, James the brother of Jesus was killed, although Acts does not mention it. By the time Luke sat down to write, both Peter and Paul had been martyred along with countless others in Rome. These events were probably in Luke's mind when he reported Paul's relationships with civil authorities in general and with the Roman Caesar in particular. The material Luke provides is of two kinds: reports of Paul's "scrapes with the law" and speeches made in defense of himself and of the Christian movement. Both merit attention.

The first "run-in" with the law which Luke describes is in 16:16-40, the famous story of Paul in Philippi. The situation was triggered by the impact of the gospel on a local business: A slave girl could no longer be used to tell fortunes. But the incident itself is allowed to fade out of the picture because it is not important for Luke's purpose. His main interest is the charge against Paul. It is the old Roman fear of new religion (16:20f.). This is the real issue. Because Paul accepted the punishment, it was not until morning that the authorities learned that they themselves had broken a law to enforce a custom — they had beaten a Roman citizen. Luke's concern with the story is not simply to tell about the earthquake that broke up a prayer-meeting in jail, nor is it simply the conversion of the jailer; he is also making a strong plea throughout the entire story for what we would call "due process of law."

Things were no better for Paul at the next stop, Thessalonica (17:1-9). Here too, the emotions of the crowd were fanned and this time a clear charge of subversion was made — these men were carrying on "un-Roman activities." So they were hailed into court with this charge: "These men who have turned the world upside down have come here also, and Jason has received them [that is, they are 'outside agitators' who have perverted a local citizen]; and they are all acting against the decrees of Caesar, saying that there is another king, Jesus." The comment that the city fathers "were disturbed when they heard this" is doubtless the understatement of the book! For some reason, Luke does not report how Paul replied to the charge. Perhaps this is because he reserves all speeches of self-defense for the last part of the book.

The turning-point in Paul's career takes place in Ephesus. Here, according to Acts, is where the third phase of his career begins (19:21ff.). As in Philippi, the preaching of the gospel had unfavorable consequences for local business. Here the conversions to Christianity were so numerous that they ruined the sale of silver statues of the city goddess. The leaders of the "depressed industry" held a meeting to discuss the crisis, and the issue was put very clearly: The goddess was in danger, and therefore the city was threatened (19:23-27). Declining business was only a symptom of the disease. Here we see clearly how religion, business, and patriotism are interwoven. To threaten the worship of the goddess would not only affect the economy but would endanger the security of the community. We can understand why the alarmed citizens cried out eagerly "Great is Artemis" (or Diana). Here is a frenzied profession of allegiance which is intended to safeguard the city by letting Artemis know that they are really loyal. When the situation turned into a riot in the amphitheater, a city official quieted the mob by reminding them that Ephesus was indeed the protector of the worship of Artemis, and that any complaints against Paul could be taken up by the courts. Under no circumstances were law and order to break down.

Luke tells the story in great detail because he has a double interest in it. First, he uses it to initiate the third section of Acts, which is dominated by the problem of Paul's relationship to the state and to civil authorities. Hence, this story initiates the whole section. It is a symbol of the whole. Second, he begins this section by recounting another appeal for judicial procedure and for justice in the courts instead of mob action.

As the story of Paul moves toward its climax, Luke reports that in Jerusalem Paul was the victim of just such a mob (21:27ff). The Roman officer arrested him to put him into protective custody, and brought him to the barracks. Here Paul informed him that there was a case of mistaken identity; he was not the Egyptian Jew who had tried to lead a revolt (21:37ff.). This detail reminds the reader again that neither Jesus nor Paul nor any Christians were political revolutionaries, even though Palestine was beginning to seethe with Jewish "Freedom Fighters" against Rome. This exchange on the steps of the barracks allows Luke to report a long speech in which Paul outlines his relation to Judaism. Before the scene is over, Luke makes still another point — that Paul is a Roman citizen whose rights deserve to be respected. Here again, Luke protests against illegal action against Christians.

From this point on, Chapters 22-26 consist mostly of speeches made in self-defense. Throughout, we see Paul proclaiming his innocence, the Roman army's repeated efforts to rescue Paul from the Jews (just as Pilate had tried to save Jesus), and the climax in which the puppet king (Agrippa) and the Roman governor agree that "this man could have been set free if he had not appealed to Caesar" (26:32). Nowhere in Acts is the political innocence of Christianity more clearly stated. At the same time, the appeal to Caesar shows that Paul is not a renegade, but a man so convinced of his innocence that he is unafraid to make such an appeal. No anarchist or insurrectionist would do so. It rests on the assumption that even if judicial process in the provinces is slow (Paul had been in jail two years now), surely Caesar himself would render justice with dispatch.

Then follows the famous sea voyage to Rome, climaxed by

a shipwreck (27:1-28:10). Even this story serves Luke's aim: Paul is shown as a model prisoner who actually made it possible for all prisoners to be brought safely to Rome. Luke is quietly pointing out: "See, even as prisoners, and innocent ones at that, the Christians are not like the others, but are acting like responsible citizens."

The end of Acts has long puzzled Luke's readers. But, even here, the author deals with the problems of church and state, for he implies that this innocent Paul was unmolested in Rome (28:30f.). Therefore his death must not be regarded as an act of injustice, an event in which Rome degraded herself.

We may summarize what Luke has shown us. (1) Christianity is a religion and not a political movement. Neither its founder nor its leaders are revolutionaries who agitate from place to place. (2) Christians are law-abiding citizens and subjects of Rome who respect the authority of the state. As citizens and subjects, they claim equal protection under law, no more and no less. (3) Even so, Christians know where their ultimate allegiance lies — it is with God and Christ, the true Lord and King. The supreme sovereign for the Christian is not the state but the Savior. In light of what Luke has shown us about the Christians of his generation, we are driven to rethink our own situation. It would be a mistake, of course, to assume that Acts has defined fully the Christian position, for Acts does not speak for the whole New Testament, nor for all time. "The Christian position" is hammered out on the scene, from generation to generation. Nevertheless, Acts does point us to certain essentials, and these demand attention.

CHRISTIAN WITNESS OR CIVIC RELIGION?

We may begin to ponder the issues raised by Acts by asking a question: On what basis can the Christian be a good citizen of his country? The answer seems fairly simple for most Americans, because the government is friendly to religion in general and to Christianity in particular. We are led to believe that the Christian can easily be a loyal citizen because the state is friendly to the faith. But what about the Christian who lives in a country whose government has a different attitude toward Chrisianity? For example, how can a Christian in Burma be a good citizen of his country, which wants to be a Buddhist nation with toleration for Christians? On what basis can a believer be a good citizen of India, which is Hindu, or a good citizen of Egypt, which is Moslem, or of Czechoslovakia, which is communist? As a matter of fact, is the basis on which Christians are good citizens in those countries any different from the basis on which we are loyal citizens of the United States? Theologically speaking, the answer is No, because the Christian's attitude toward his government is not determined by the government's attitude toward Christianity, but rather by his own faith in the lordship of Jesus. What is decisive is not the government's policy toward the Christian religion but the meaning of Jesus' lordship in relation to political allegiance.

Ordinarily, we do not see much relationship between what we believe about Jesus and our attitude toward the government under which we live. We tend to regard our beliefs about Jesus as a matter of faith, and our citizenship as a matter of civics or politics. Actually, however, what we believe about Jesus has decisive results for the way we understand all governmental authority, and it is the aim of the next few paragraphs to make this point clear.

The starting point for the Christian understanding of Jesus is his resurrection. In the New Testament, as can be seen in the writings of Paul, for example, this is the center of gravity. Precisely what the resurrection means depends partly on the situation in which we think about it; in other words, the questions we ask about the meaning of the resurrection shape the answers it gives. In this way, as we ask our questions, Jesus' resurrection comes to have a whole range of meanings.

One of the basic affirmations about Jesus' resurrection is

that this means Jesus is next to God. The ancient creeds of the church put it in more familiar words: "seated at the right hand of God the Father Almighty." In the New Testament, the resurrection was understood as exalting him to this place of authority and not simply as recalling him to life. At first glance, believing that Jesus is next to God looks harmless enough, and seems far removed from political matters. But, given an appropriate issue, this conviction becomes dangerous.

Because Jesus is next to God, faith in Jesus is really a commitment to him as an absolute authority, a supreme sovereign. No other sovereignty can compete, because only Jesus was exalted to this status of being next to God. Whoever holds this belief firmly enough to commit his life to the consequences, finds that every other allegiance must be secondary to this one. In other words, the Christian is involved in a radical commitment to an absolute. Christianity is a totalitarian faith. It is a commitment with ultimate consequences because it is a commitment of one's self to Jesus who is next to God. To put it colloquially, for Jesus to be lord means that he alone is "boss" around here, and that no one else can ever be more than "straw boss" — no person and no state. Seeing this authority clearly is essential for all Christian political thinking and acting.

Let us be specific. It is one of the great achievements of the American system that the government has made a place for those citizens who reject its authority to send them to war or to salute the flag, because of religious convictions or conscience. For the government to tolerate this defiance of governmental authority (for this is what it amounts to) is an achievement for which every Christian should be grateful, whether he claims such toleration for himself or marches to war. But being grateful does not mean that he must make the American system absolute, ultimate, that it shall become his God.

The Christian who will go to boot camp can defend the Christian who prefers a C.O. camp because, even though the two take differing courses of action, both recognize that they are united in this one thing: top allegiance to Christ. There may be vigorous discussion as to whether wearing the uniform is a mark of responsibility or of compromise, but there is no disagreement as to the place of ultimate loyalty. Regardless of particular conclusions or courses of action, the Christian is convinced that political loyalty is never more than secondary allegiance, because the first goes to Christ. The state, any state and any government, can never hold more than second mortgage on the Christian's loyalty, because faith gives Jesus the first.

The particular flag under which the believer may be living does not affect this loyalty. The basic allegiance of the Christian to Christ is required equally in the USA and the USSR. In this light, the difference between Washington and Moscow is that Washington accepts this priority without impugning the citizen's standing while Moscow does not. Moscow's attitude still leads to pressures and even persecutions against him; Washington's leads to religious slogans on pennies, and to chaplains in the armed services. Actually, however, neither government's attitude affects the inner structure of a Christian's allegiance to Christ.

This general understanding is very important as we face particular issues. All around the world, the key word is revolution. It may be in Cuba or China, North Africa or South America. Wherever the Christian finds himself, he must make decisions with regard to these revolutions, for or against particular government policies. Often he must decide whether to support the government under which he was born or to support a revolution which will give birth to another one. In such situations, choices are as difficult as they are inevitable.

In the security of the United States, where political change takes place peacefully through elections, it is difficult to give advice to believers caught by revolutions. We will restrict ourselves to one basic point, which is as important for American attitudes as it is for believers' actions in Congo or Korea. The point is simply that for the Christian to regard himself as a loyal citizen of his country, wherever it is, does not require him to resist all change. Loyalty to his country does not mean that he must defend the status quo; in fact, it may lead him to press for radical changes. For example, loyalty to Germany and to the meaning of Christ led Dietrich Bonhoeffer to participate in the plot to kill Hitler.

Because the Christian's loyalties are graded in such a way that top allegiance is given only to God in Christ, he regards every state and every government as living under God's judgment. This relationship is just as true for those governments which enjoy the official blessing of a church, as in Spain or Sweden, as it is for Soviet Russia which proclaims itself to be atheistic. The Christian who genuinely believes that the resurrection has exalted Jesus to a position next to God sees that the Russian claim to be atheistic is theologically irrelevant. The Christian's view is no more affected by what Russian atheists say about God than his belief about the shape of the earth is affected by some crackpot who says the earth is flat. The Christian believes every state is under God's judgment, regardless of that state's policy toward religion.[7]

Armed with this conviction, each Christian makes his decisions regarding his own government on the basis of his considered assessment of whether this government adequately reflects God's will for that time and place or not. His particular decision, to support a revolution or to oppose it, to participate in government affairs or not, depends not on the ability to find a Bible verse telling him what to do, but on his theological convictions (grounded in the total biblical faith) as he brings them to bear on the problems at hand. In such a situation, there can be no purely right answers, but only answers with varying degrees of error. The Christian's decisions are no less under judgment than the state itself.

In light of this insight, we may recall that Acts shows us something very important for our time — that wherever the gospel goes, there is conflict — a conflict of interest and a conflict of convictions. We must not always assume that the gospel is a pacifier for mankind to suck in times of distress. It is also a fire and a sword. We must not interpret Acts to mean that Christians are always politically quiet simply because the church is not a revolutionary party. Just the opposite is true: Because the church is not a political party, its impact is not restricted to the realignment of the government, but affects the economy as well. In our society, which is dominated by business, we need to ponder the fact that in Acts it was the businessmen who were offended by the results of the gospel before the police were.

To be blunt, our basic temptation is to abuse Acts by reading it as if it were a scriptural warrant for resisting social and economic change, as if it were a mandate to be disengaged. We must remember that Luke's point is made in light of growing political pressure. The kind of situation which we Christians in America face, a democracy in which we share responsibility for government policy and social change, never occurred to Luke. His "quietism" cannot be made the absolute standard for us. Acts, however, does tell us to expect conflicts wherever the gospel strikes root. The exact nature of the conflicts depends on the place where they occur, but conflict is inevitable, whether it be with the medicine man who is protecting a primitive idea of medicine in the jungle or with a local "priest" of the John Birch Society who is guarding an America which doesn't exist either.[8] Because in our time we find ourselves without the serenity of Christendom, the conflicts with state and society will probably increase wherever the gospel is believed. The totality of the gospel is confronting the totalitarianism of the state, for, as Christopher Dawson has rightly observed, today every state is totalitarian.[9]

The struggle with communism complicates our situation

and summons us to be doubly alert. The danger of the church in our century is not simply the threat of martyrdom if the communists win. The choice is not one of safety if we win, peril if they do. We Christians also face real danger if the West should win, and we face it right now as we struggle to survive. This danger consists of being made into the state religion, of waking up to learn that, like the priests of pagan Rome, we are expected to perform the rituals of the church in order to preserve the state. Even though we are leaving Christendom behind, it is quite possible that in growing desperation the public or government will say to the church, "Guarantee our survival or be replaced by a religion that will." This can be a very subtle demand. In fact, it is even promoted by preachers of the gospel who promise that, if America will turn to Christ, she will survive and win. The gospel cannot promise this result without ceasing to be the gospel.

Sometimes this attitude is not so subtle, but becomes an out-and-out appeal for a Christian crusade against communism. Those who are ready to heed such a call forget that, during the Middle Ages, the church launched crusades against the Turks (they called them the "infidel" Turks as we speak of "atheistic" communists) for several hundred years, and that the whole project was a travesty on the gospel and a military fiasco. They forget that, theologically speaking (and for the Christian this is determinative), there is no basis on which a *Christian* crusade can be launched against communism or any other -ism. If Christians participate in crusades (for example, Eisenhower's "Crusade in Europe" against Hitler) it is because they have decided that warring against Nazi power is less evil than the consequences of not going to war. There is, moreover, the whole tradition of the so-called "just war" — a position which insists that some wars are just, while others (for sheer imperialistic expansion) are not. Such considerations, which are not to be ruled out, often stem more from prudential than from theological considerations. They are, however, made somewhat obsolete by nuclear weapons. In any case, as far as "atheistic" communists are concerned, Jesus did not send us to *crusade against* them but to *witness to* them. Whoever thinks, as a Christian acting on clear Christian grounds, that he must *crusade* against communism has already sold out to Satan, for he is saying (a) that the resurrection did not make Jesus Lord over all, and that therefore his lordship stops at the Soviet border, and (b) that Jesus' lordship is going to be established by the sword wielded by Christian crusaders. Such a sellout is really a closeout sale, for it puts the Christian witness out of business altogether.[10]

In short, we are in danger of thinking that we are living in times characterized by Romans 13, when actually we are slipping into the era marked by Revelation 13. Already the land is being filled with priests, pagan and Christian alike, who bid us worship the beast. Note carefully the following words:

> We want a vital national Church that will express all the spiritual forces of our people. . . . We want the reawakened American sense of vitality respected in our Church. We want to make our Church a vital force. In the fateful struggle for the freedom and future of America the Church in its administration has proven weak. Hitherto the Church has not called for an all-out fight against atheistic Marxism. . . . We want our Church to be in the forefront of the crucial battle for the existence of our people. . . . We demand that . . . a fight be waged against a Marxism which is enemy of religion and the nation and against its Christian social fellow travelers of every shade. . . . We miss a confident daring for God and for the mission of the Church. The way into the Kingdom of God is through struggle, cross, and sacrifice, not through a false peace. . . . We want an evangelical Church that is rooted in our nationhood. We repudiate the spirit of a Christian world-citizenship.[11]

Far too many American Christians agree with these sentiments entirely. But they may not realize that these words were taken from the "Guiding Principles" of the "German Christians" who worked with Hitler to make the church into a slave of the state. In the quotation only the word "German" was changed to "American."

All around us are forces that demand that the church shout "Great is Artemis of the Ephesians!" — that is, that ministers go into the pulpits Sunday after Sunday to proclaim the American God and their hatred of communism. Such men are unwitting priests of the state who bid us put incense on Caesar's altar because Caesar is putting incense on ours through tax exemptions and slogans on dollar bills. The only way for the church in America to avoid becoming the American Church is for a reassessment of its allegiance, and for a willingness to compromise the claim of Christ with no one. Only then can Christians be free to be Christian citizens.

John's Gospel reports that during Jesus' trial, the Jerusalem crowd bellowed its patriotism by shouting, "We have no king but Caesar." The Book of Acts shows the Christian alternative: "There is another king, Jesus." Here the Christian must take his stand, "come Hell or high water." In our time, he may face both.

NOTES

1. In this book, "text" always refers to the Bible, never to the words of this or any other book *about* the Bible.

CHAPTER ONE

*From *Theology Between Yesterday and Tomorrow,* by Joseph L. Hromadka. Copyright © 1957, W. L. Jenkins. The Westminster Press, page 59.

**From *Understanding the Bible,* by Fred J. Denbeaux. Copyright © 1958, W. L. Jenkins. The Westminster Press, page 93.

1. It is generally understood that Christendom was born in the time of Constantine, the first Christian emperor. He made Sunday a legal day of rest for all except farmers (in A.D. 321). This marks the beginning of the legal Christianization of society. Sixty years later, Emperor Theodosius made Christianity the official religion of the empire. For sixteen centuries, Europe generally assumed that being a citizen meant being a Christian.

2. Leo Pfeffer has illustrated this clearly: "American Protestantism conceives the ideal society as one in which everybody is sober and diligent, shuns gambling, and scrupulously observes the Sabbath, whereas American Catholicism conceives it as one from which moderate consumption of liquors and moderate engaging in games of chance are not excluded, but wherein everyone shuns birth control and has large families. Each would willingly employ the instrumentality of law and government to achieve its conception of the ideal society. That, of course, is what is meant by competition among religious cultures." *Creeds in Competition* (New York: Harper and Row, 1958), page 99.

3. Professor Littell has recently been arguing that we are not in a post-Christian but a pre-Christian period; that, when measured by the degree of Christianization in depth, the population in

America is being Christianized the way it is on those mission fields where the church has to deal with mass conversions. This stimulating book has many keen insights; yet I believe the author has missed an essential point, namely, that the question of the post-Christian period deals with the impact of Christianity on the general stream of the culture and its values, not on the number of Christians who take their faith seriously. In American history, the church had more impact on the life of society at a time when only a small percentage of the population were churchmen. Franklin Littell, *From State Church to Pluralism* (Garden City: Doubleday Anchor Book, 1962).

4. This is the reason why some writers speak of our time as the "post-Christian era." Those who speak of our era in these terms use the phrase to describe the things we have been noting—that Christianity no longer serves as the most significant shaper of society and its values. The phrase "post-Christian" is a historian's way of describing our culture. The theologian, of course, may agree completely with this description while at the same time insisting that this decline of the church's position in our culture in no way affects the lordship of Christ theologically. The lordship of Christ depends on the resurrection, not on the relative influence churchmen might have. The church does not make Jesus Lord by increasing its power; the influence of Christianity on society is the impact of the church which lives in a particular way because it believes Jesus is Lord, whether society as a whole is impressed by this belief or not. We will return to this again.

5. Paul Ramsey, "Preface." Gabriel Vahanian, *The Death of God* (New York: George Braziller, Inc., 1961), page xiii.

6. A simple way of seeing this is to remember what happens during the Christmas season. It is not the church which determines how the last weeks of December are spent; instead, the merchants shape the way the church will observe the birth of Jesus (e.g., entering floats in Christmas parades). In contrast, three hundred years ago in New England it was against the law to celebrate Christmas at all because the church regarded it as a sin. This reversal of roles with regard to Christmas reflects what has happened in the intervening generations. For a brief statement of how even the modern Christmas affects the lives of those who have no religious reason to celebrate it, see Pfeffer's remarks in *Creeds in Competition*, pages 1-6.

7. For a fuller discussion of this approach to the Bible, see my book, *Taking the Bible Seriously* (New York: Association Press, 1962).

8. Since Luke and Acts belong together, it is obvious that they were separated (by the Gospel According to John) only for some compelling reason. It is not hard to find: Luke belongs with the first three gospels, while John is unique in almost every way and so is placed last among the four. Moreover, Acts serves to bridge the Gospels and the Epistles. It probably received its present title when the two volumes were separated. No one knows what the writer himself called his two-volume set.

9. It is important to note that this controversy is NOT an example of modernist intrigues against the Bible, for the Bible itself never identifies the author of Acts. This is a scientific problem of determining the author on the basis of evidence. Theologically liberal and conservative scholars are found on both sides, because they assess the facts differently.

10. Students of Acts sometimes talk of these passages as being quotations from a diary, but there is no evidence that he was copying—he could just as well have been remembering.

11. Morton Enslin has summarized this point well in *Christian Beginnings* (New York: Harper and Row, 1938), page 420: "Professor Cadbury has . . . completely exploded this fallacy of the alleged medical language in Luke-Acts by demonstrating that there was no technical phraseology available for the ancient physician, comparable to that of the present-day medical jargon, and by showing that all the words and phrases eagerly pounced upon by Hobart and his pedissequi were in common use by such writers as Aristophanes and Lucian, who, to say the least, had never received a doctor's degree. Were it not for the accidental reference of Paul to 'Luke, the beloved physician,' it is extremely possible that the famous but enigmatic author might have come down to us not in doctor's robes, but in the garb of a sea captain." A wise-cracking student tried to combine these possibilities by suggesting that the author was a ship's doctor!

12. For a variety of reasons far too complex to discuss here, most scholars place Luke-Acts in the last quarter of the first century, probably around A.D. 85. Those who think Acts was written while Paul was still alive (very few scholars) must, of course, date it in the early sixties. I am persuaded that any date before A.D. 70 is without adequate foundation.

13. In this connection, we should also read passages such as Acts 20:17-38 (especially v. 29f.); 1 Timothy 4:1-5; 5:17-22; 2 Timothy 2:14-26; Titus 1:5-16; 2 Peter 2:1-3; 1 John 4:1-6. All of these passages may be dated relatively late in the New Testament period; they disclose the interrelatedness of doctrine and leadership because people who could not agree theologically often challenged the leaders of the church.

14. No one knows anything about Theophilus other than what can be inferred from the prefaces to Luke and Acts, and this is almost nothing. Though a variety of suggestions have been made, we simply do not know who Theophilus was.

15. The structure of the Book of Acts is not altogether clear, largely because so many different pieces of material went into it. Many students find a hint of the outline in the geographical movement in 1:8, ". . . witnesses in Jerusalem, and in all Judea and Samaria and to the end of the earth." There is no doubt that the story roughly follows this general scheme. But this outline does not reflect clearly enough Luke's own intent in telling the story just the way he does. That is, it is an outline of *what* he tells but gives no real clue to *why* he tells it just this way. The outline we are suggesting here attempts to locate Luke's own interest more clearly. This purpose will become clear as we proceed.

We may also recall that Luke divided his gospel into three sections as well. Mark, it will be remembered, divided the ministry of Jesus into two parts, Galilee and Jerusalem (Chapters 1-9 and 10-16). But Luke divided it into the following: Galilee (3:1-9:50); the journey to Jerusalem (9:51-18:30) and Jerusalem (18:31-24:52).

16. There is some evidence that Paul was released, went to Spain as he had originally intended (Romans 15:22-29) and was again imprisoned and finally martyred. Those who believe that Paul wrote the Pastoral Epistles, as a few scholars still do, must hold that Paul was released because there is simply no other way to include the travels of Paul reflected here (*e.g.*, Titus 1:5) into the course of his life. Since it is virtually impossible to regard these letters, at least in their present form, as genuine letters of Paul, they cannot be used to establish a release and second imprisonment. A careful sifting of the available evidence leads to the conclusion that we know only that Paul was martyred in Rome. Everything beyond this is an inference.

CHAPTER TWO

*From *Theology Between Yesterday and Tomorrow*, by Joseph L. Hromadka, page 58.

1. The R.S.V. puts "and was carried up into heaven" in the footnote rather than the text, because the best manuscripts do not include it.

2. The word "Christ" is the English way of saying *Christos*, which is the Greek translation of "Messiah," just as *Christus* is the Latin equivalent. The Latin translation would be *Unctus* (as in the Catholic sacrament of Unction).

3. The most famous effort was the church's lobbying on behalf of Prohibition. The problems, theological as well as legal, that this movement produced, are well known. Leo Pfeffer points out the problem involved in the effort to make one kind of Protestant ethic (abstinence) the law of a pluralistic society. Protestants, he says, have no hesitation to ask the government to force all people into abstinence, but get excited when Catholics ask the same government to prevent birth control information and means from circulating (*Creeds in Competition*, page 98). Actually, from both a religious and a legal point of view, these are matters for the disciplined consciences of the two religious groups; asking the government and the police to manage the morals for the church is really a form of avoiding responsibility.

4. It has been suggested that Luke adjusted the story to make his point, that the people were Gentiles, not Jews. If so, this would mean that the original story told how the gospel was immediately and symbolically proclaimed to all mankind. The theory rests partly on the list of places mentioned (and omitted) from the passage. This list has not yet been explained satisfactorily. Under these circumstances, it is best to let the story remain as it stands and leave open the question of the way the story may have read when Luke learned it.

5. Some interpreters have argued that Luke is changing the idea of tongues. Originally, speaking in tongues meant a kind of pentecostalism, the sort of thing Paul tried to channel and control among his Corinthian converts (see 1 Corinthians 12-14). Luke, it is said, interpreted "speaking in tongues" as speaking foreign tongues, that is, foreign languages. This interpretation has much to commend it.

6. For Paul himself, "the Lord" and "the Spirit" are so closely re-lated that they could be used almost interchangeably at times. See the way "you are in the Spirit" (and "the Spirit in you") alternates with "Christ in you" in Romans 8:9-11. See also the famous statement in 2 Corinthians 3:17.

7. This is partly because there is a contradiction between our language (which requires us to speak of Spirit as "it") and our doctrine (which requires us to speak of God as "he").

8. The doctrine of the Trinity grapples with the knotty issues raised here, for theologians have long recognized that clear thinking about the Spirit leads to trinitarian conclusions. When we speak of God as Creator or Father, we refer to his role as source of the universe and to his sovereignty over it. God's work as Savior is centered in Jesus of Nazareth. The Spirit is understood as God personally present with us. These are not three gods (some sort of divine committee) but the one God who is known in these three distinguishable ways.

9. John's Gospel points in the same direction when it reports that Jesus will send the Spirit from the Father; when he comes, he will witness to the Son (15:26). In the same vein, this writing says that the Father will send the Spirit in the name of the Son and that his mission will be to bring to remembrance the mission (and hence the meaning) of Jesus (14:26). "Remembrance" here means more than sheer recollection.

CHAPTER THREE

*Gabriel Vahanian, *The Death of God*, pages 184-185.

1. From *The Nazarene Gospel Restored* by Robert Graves and Joshua Podro. Copyright 1953 by Robert Graves and Joshua Podro. Reprinted by permission of Doubleday & Company, Inc., New York, and A. P. Watt & Son, London, Cassell & Co., Ltd., London, and International Authors, N. V. Page 14.

2. It is essential to approach all the speeches and sermons in Acts properly. None of them should be regarded as a stenographer's transcript. They do not give us a word-for-word report, but the gist of what was said. This is clear from the fact that they are too short to be genuine speeches. Furthermore, Luke gives the clue to all the speeches when he says the first one is not reported verbatim: "And he testified with many other words and exhorted them. . . ." (Acts 2:40). Moreover, since the author felt free

to summarize the speeches, he presented them in a way that reveals what he regarded important in them for his own time. In this way, the speaker could address the later reader more directly; thus Luke allowed Peter and Paul to speak to his own generation what he believed was the heart of the apostolic message. That Luke has his reader in mind more than the original audience is clear from the emphases of the speeches, and especially from the details. For example, Acts 1:15-26 reports the election of Matthias to succeed Judas Iscariot. Peter began the proceedings by making a speech in which he reported what happened to Judas. But, in Jerusalem, Aramaic-speaking Peter would not have spoken these exact words: "And it became known to all the inhabitants of Jerusalem, so that the field was called in *their* language Akeldama, that is, Field of Blood." This detail is for the benefit of the readers who do not understand what "Akeldama" means and who do not live in Jerusalem. The speeches and sermons, then, are digests of what Luke believed was said, stylized to show their current significance. This characteristic does not mean that the sermons are sheer inventions; they are too clearly filled with expressions that look like translations from Aramaic or Hebrew and with concepts which appear typical of the early Palestinian church to be regarded as imitations. They probably rest on traditions and memories of the sort of things the apostles used to say. The best discussion of the speeches and sermons in Acts is by Martin Dibelius in *Studies in the Acts of the Apostles,* trans. by Mary Ling (New York: Scribner's, 1956).

3. It should be clear that by news that is "good" we do not mean news that is simply pleasant or reassuring. Rather, by "good" news we mean an announcement which contains a message dealing effectively with the fundamental problem of man before God and with his neighbor. It is news of what God has done for man.

4. Quoted from M. R. James, *The Apocryphal New Testament,* (Oxford: Clarendon Press, 1953), rev. ed. (my italics). Peter, of course, had nothing to do with this document which circulated in his name during the second century.

5. Rudolf Bultmann has made this point many times; for example in his famous essay, "New Testament and Mythology," he writes: "The grace of God means *the forgiveness of sin,* and brings deliverance from the bondage of the past. The old quest for visible security, the hankering after tangible realities, and the clinging to transitory objects, is sin, for by it we shut out invisible reality

... and refuse God's future which comes to us as a gift. But once we open our hearts to the grace of God, our sins are forgiven; we are released from the past." Quoted from Reginald H. Fuller's translation of *Kerygma and Myth* (London: S.P.C.K., 1953), page 19.

6. In this matter of forgiveness and repentance, Calvin is to be followed more than popular Arminianism. Thus Calvin clearly insisted that repentance is the result of faith: "There are some, however, who suppose that repentance precedes faith, rather than flows from it, or is produced by it as fruit from a tree. Such persons have never known the power of repentance, and are moved to feel this way by an unduly slight argument" (*Institutes* III 3:1). He rightly sees that the real meaning of the theme of Jesus' preaching is a summons to repent because the Kingdom has come near. Calvin provides a clear definition of repentance: ". . . it is the true turning of our life to God, a turning that arises from a pure and earnest fear of him; and it consists in the mortification of our flesh and of the old man, and in the vivification of the Spirit" (III 3:5). To make it perfectly clear that repentance does not mean preliminary regret, he says "I interpret repentance as regeneration, whose sole end is to restore in us the image of God . . ." (III 3:8). Calvin made these assertions in the face of the same sort of popular misunderstanding as is common today; in particular, he was opposing those who required a period of repentance before accepting men into the church: "I am speaking of very many of the Anabaptists, especially those who marvellously exult in being spiritual; and of their companions, the Jesuits, and like dregs. Obviously, that giddy spirit brings forth such fruits that it limits to a paltry few days a repentance that for the Christian man ought to extend throughout his life" (III 3:2). From *Calvin: Institutes of the Christian Religion*. Ed. by J. T. McNeill and trans. by Ford Lewis Battles. Copyright © 1960, W. L. Jenkins. Used by permission of The Westminster Press, Phila., and The SCM Press, London.

7. This is the logical name for this story; to call it the parable of the prodigal son is to deflect attention from the most important feature.

CHAPTER FOUR

*From *Theology Between Yesterday and Tomorrow*, by Joseph L. Hromadka, page 60.

1. Many Jews in New Testament times used both a Gentile and a Jewish name; thus a man would be both Jason and Joshua. Doubtless Paul regarded Saul as his Jewish name. There is no reason to think he changed names when he was converted. In fact, Acts shifts the nomenclature from Saul to Paul during the first missionary tour (13:9), not at the conversion. We ought to stop referring to the conversion as the time when Saul became Paul; this is nonsense historically, and theologically as well, for conversion to Christianity brings a new name only when the old name is so pagan that it can no longer be used by the Christian. This is not the case for any Jew.

2. Quoted from the fourth-century historian Eusebius, who was quoting a second-century writer named Hegesippus. Reprinted by permission of the publishers and The Loeb Classical Library from *Eusebius: Ecclesiastical History* II 23: 3f. Translated by Kirsopp Lake, (Cambridge, Mass.: Harvard University Press, 1926), Vol. I, page 171. Roman Catholics, of course, deny that James was Jesus' brother because, according to the doctrine of the perpetual virginity of Mary, Jesus could have no brothers. They usually regard James as a cousin or half-brother of Jesus (by an earlier marriage of Joseph). The most recent, brief discussion of the problems connected with James, both in the New Testament and in Early Christian tradition, is that of William Beardslee in *The Interpreter's Dictionary of the Bible,* George Buttrick, ed. (Nashville: Abingdon Press, 1962), Vol. II, pages 790-94.

3. Acts says that "Christian" was not the original name for the believers, but it does not give any clear picture of what they called themselves at first. Perhaps they were not as interested in naming themselves as we are. One way of designating Christians, however, was "Those of the Way"—believers as those who follow a particular mode of life (see Acts 9:2; 22:4; 24:14, 22).

4. Severe penalties were given to those who cheated. The Ananias and Sapphira story in Acts 5 reflects a similar seriousness in such matters. Acts shows, however, that the church did not require the selling of property and the sharing of proceeds before baptism.

5. The "Hellenists" also appear at 9:29, where they apparently are Greek-living Jews who have not become Christians. Some inter-

preters have tried to argue that the difference between Hellenists and Hebrews was one of language, but this is too superficial
a difference to account for the tensions.

6. Many scholars believe that behind the brief report in Acts lies
the fact that there were really two wings of the church, and that
the Seven were actually leaders of the Hellenist wing rather
than financial overseers for the whole church. This interpretation would explain why the only stories we have about their
work report them doing exactly what the apostles did, only with
a different "clientele." If so (and there is much to commend
it), then Luke emphasizes the harmonious element in the situation by omitting the tensions. In his day, when the church was
becoming more and more involved in controversies, he may
well have regarded it more important to accent the positive side
of the early church than simply to describe everything that
happened. This is usually what happens in sermon illustra-
tions—the preacher accents those elements of the story which
serve his immediate purpose.

7. This Jewish missionary work, and the relation of Jesus to it,
has recently been discussed by the eminent German New Testament scholar, Joachim Jeremias, in *Jesus' Promise to the Nations* (Studies in Biblical Theology No. 24), trans. by S. H.
Hooke (Naperville, Ill.: Alec R. Allenson, Inc., 1958). See also
the article "Proselyte" by Marvin Pope in *The Interpreter's Dictionary of the Bible,* George Buttrick, ed. (Nashville: Abingdon
Press, 1962), Vol. III, pages 921-31. This article deals with the
general problem of the Gentile's relation to the Jew in the Bible.

8. One might ask why this statement does not read "God has
granted forgiveness" to the Gentiles. There is no necessary contradiction between this text and the exposition of repentance
and forgiveness in Chapter 3. We must remember that Judaism
was actively interested in winning Gentiles and that repentance
was one of the basic elements of a pagan's conversion to
Judaism. Hence it is clear that repentance followed by forgiveness was a "plan of salvation" which was already being preached
long before Jesus appeared on the scene. Thus the message of
God's forgiveness as his response to man's repentance is not
distinctively Christian at all, and in no way depends on Jesus.
On this basis our text would not really make sense in that situation at all, for no Jew doubted that God would forgive Gentiles if they repented of their paganism and worshiped the

one true God. The text makes sense only if we assume that it is a compressed statement, a capsulated formula, which omits words for the sake of brevity. The full statement would then read, "God granted them repentance as a result of his work in Jesus." Since this work is itself an expression of God's forgiving act which makes repentance (a genuine turning to God) possible, the text actually supports the interpretation of forgiveness and repentance we have been developing.

9. In ancient times, the Jews were often despised because of their refusal to participate in the whole life of the communities of the empire, but insisted on keeping their traditions. Some Jews, like the mother of Timothy (Acts 16:1-3), were more lenient, to the point of marrying Gentiles. The rabbis, on the other hand, tried to define very precisely the relations permitted with Gentiles. For example, "For three days before the festivals of the Gentiles it is forbidden to have business with them—to lend to them or to borrow from them. . . . Cattle may not be left in the inns of Gentiles since they are suspected of bestiality; nor may a woman remain alone with them since they are suspected of lewdness; nor may a man remain alone with them since they are suspected of shedding blood. The daughter of an Israelite may not assist a Gentile woman in childbirth for idolatry, but a Gentile woman may assist the daughter of an Israelite." cf. Abodah Zarah 1:1; 2:1, quoted from the *Mishnah,* trans. by Herbert Danby (Oxford: Oxford University Press, 1933), page 43f. The reasons behind such regulations were the fear of losing the Jewish identity in a sea of paganism, the fear of being made an unwitting participant in idolatry, and the fear of compromising the Jewish way of life which was regarded as willed by God.

For two reasons it is difficult to know the extent to which these regulations were enforced in the time of Jesus and Paul: (a) It is impossible to know how old the laws were by the time they were committed to writing more than a century later. Especially important is the fact that the great revolt in A.D. 66 brought a major shift in Jewish life. Getting behind this to the Jewish life known to Jesus and Paul is therefore doubly difficult.

(b) One is never certain of the extent to which these regulations were enforced. It is clear that many Palestinian Jews, like those living in Egypt or Greece, ignored them. In other words, even knowing what regulations existed in the time of

Jesus and Paul would not be enough to give us the picture we really need; what we should have is knowledge about the extent to which these things were actually done.

10. These remarks were made at the first annual race relations lecture at Vanderbilt Divinity School in February, 1962. The address, which stresses the sovereignty of God, is published as "The Starting Place in Christian Race Relations" in *Motive*, Vol. 22, May, 1962.

11. The fact that our discussion of church and race has been carried on within the perspectives of Acts does not mean that this is the only thing to be said on the subject. What Acts says (and shows) is worth hearing, even though by itself it is not an adequate Christian approach. Its limitations are apparent in the fact that it accents the reluctance of the church to enter into fellowship with Gentiles without portraying strongly enough the genuine joys of discovering that the Gentile was really a brother and that the earlier fears were unfounded. The realism of Acts is remarkable, for there is no reason to doubt that the early church was reluctant at first to accept fully persons of another race and culture. One would seriously misuse Acts if he took this material as scriptural warrant for sullen compliance with desegregation. The motive underlying the analysis of this chapter has not been to provide biblical excuses for reluctance and resistance to desegregation, but to suggest that events of our own time, like those of the first-generation Christians, are pulling the church faster than it is willing to go. If we are able to say that the course of events reported in Acts was the result of God's Spirit, can we avoid asking whether the church today is not under the same divine pressure? It is not the reluctance of early Christians, but the final result, that is the norm for us.

12. Christopher Dawson, *The Historic Reality of Christian Culture* (New York: Harper and Row, 1960), page 70. The influence of Christianity on Europe has been sketched by Herbert Butterfield in *Christianity in European History* (London and New York: Oxford University Press, 1951).

13. Gabriel Vahanian has rightly observed (*The Death of God*, page 139): "*Theologically*, no age, no culture, no nation, no society is Christian, just as no man *is* but *becomes* a Christian, continually" [his italics]. From this, however, he draws the

wrong conclusion about our culture, for seen *theologically* every culture is *pre*-Christian until the Messianic Age (symbolized by the Second Coming), not post-Christian. The term "post-Christian" refers to the degree of decisive impact of the Christian faith on the culture; it is a term of sociology and history, not theology. Vahanian, unfortunately, does not see this clearly enough.

CHAPTER FIVE

*From *Religion and the Christian Faith* by Hendrik Kraemer. Published 1957, by The Westminster Press, page 450. Used by permission.

**From *Theology Between Yesterday and Tomorrow*, by Joseph L. Hromadka, page 84. The word "struggle" is romanized here for emphasis.

***Amos Wilder, "Social Symbol and the Communication of the Gospel," *Christianity and Crisis*, Volume 20, December 12, 1960, page 182.

1. Hendrik Kraemer, *op. cit.*, page 20.

2. It is unfortunate that those who work on college campuses are under constant pressure to avoid doing just this task, for many churchmen seem to assume that the student pastor's job is to sell traditional Christianity along with chili on Sunday nights. Well-meaning Christians ought rather to trust these men to help students discover for themselves the significance of vital Christian faith. This purpose often requires flexibility in method and tolerance in theological matters. It is not a matter of "watering down" the gospel, but of being patient enough to meet students where they are in order to lead them forward. Far too often, churches are more concerned that the students come home with the right answers than that they discover the cutting-edge of the faith in their own experience. In the last analysis, orthodox answers to questions asked only superficially are useless compared to creative answers which students have hammered out in their own minds to meet the driving issues.

3. For a general discussion of these materials and their meaning for Christianity, see W. C. van Unnik, *Newly Discovered Gnostic Writings* (Studies in Biblical Theology No. 30), trans. by Hubert Hoskins. (Naperville, Ill.: Alec R. Allenson, Inc., 1960). The

newly-found Gospel of Thomas (the Gospel of Thomas which reports the adventures of the boy Jesus in school is another document) with its 114 sayings (no incidents) is available in paperback, with commentary, in the book by R. M. Grant and D. N. Freedman, *The Secret Sayings of Jesus* (Garden City: Doubleday, 1960). Grant has recently published a book which contains the most important Christian Gnostic literature. Difficult as some of this is to understand, reading in this volume is rewarding because it puts one into direct contact with the most important internal rival of mainstream Christianity of the period. R. M. Grant, *Gnosticism* (New York: Harper and Row, 1961).

4. A famous example is the phrase "of one substance." The Gnostics were the first to use it, but did so to express the relation between the savior and the saved—that is, that salvation was possible because the soul of the savior was "of one substance" (made of the same stuff) as the souls of the saved. When the smoke had cleared from the anti-Gnostic battles, Christians were using the word to express the relation of the Son of God to the Father, thus using it to underline the full deity of God's Son. This word became the pivotal term in the great debates which resulted eventually in the Nicene Creed. The life story of this word in Christianity is a case history of its Christianization.

5. For a good bird's-eye view of Greek religion, see the article "Greek Religion" by Frank W. Beare in *The Interpreter's Dictionary of the Bible,* George Buttrick, ed. (Nashville: Abingdon Press, 1962), Vol. II, pages 487-500.

6. The *functional* character of theological language, especially in connection with words for salvation, is clearly seen in the following passage from a second-century Christian teacher, Clement of Alexandria (Egypt): We need "the Guide, for we are wandering; Him who gives light, for we are blind; the life-giving Spring, for we are parched with thirst. . . . We are in need of Life, for we are dead; of the Shepherd, for we are sheep; of the Educator, for we are children." Quoted from *Christ the Educator,* I, 9:83, trans. by Simon P. Wood, C.P., in *The Fathers of the Church,* Vol. 23 (New York: Fathers of the Church, Inc., 1954), page 74.

7. No English translation can catch the punch of this misunderstanding, because English nouns have no gender. But Greek

nouns, like French and German, do; the word "resurrection" is a feminine noun, *anastasis*. This means that Luke says the Athenians thought Paul was talking about a male deity (Jesus) and his female companion (Resurrection)! This kind of religious myth was widespread in the ancient world.

8. Acts mentions the Epicureans also. In this era, the clear distinctions between various kinds of philosophies has been rubbed smooth. Differences still existed, but were no longer sharply defined. Since the sermon is slanted more toward street-corner Stoicism, we are not violating the text by restricting ourselves to the Stoic problem. We must point out, however, that the Epicureans had no place for any life beyond death, since they held that death dissolved the soul forever.

9. The King James Version translates a manuscript tradition which reads "made of one *blood*"; the R.S.V. follows a better set of manuscripts which omit "blood." At some point, copyists felt that "made of one" was not clear (one what?) and inserted the word "blood." But it is obvious that the R.S.V. translates the right form of the text, not simply because the best manuscripts have it this way but because this fits the two-directional character of the sermon. The word can mean "one thing" or "one man." The Stoic would hear this as "made of one thing" (substance) and the biblically oriented reader (and Paul himself) would see it as a reference to "made of one man"—Adam.

10. The R.S.V. reads "commands all men everywhere to repent," because it follows a different manuscript tradition.

11. 1 Corinthians 1:18-2:16. There is no evidence that when Paul wrote these words he had the Athenian experience in his mind. Paul doubtless had similar receptions elsewhere; in fact, since Luke regards Mars Hill as typical, this meaning is exactly what he wants to convey.

12. James E. Sellers, *The Outsider and the Word of God* (Nashville: Abingdon Press, 1961), page 57. This book is an interestingly written analysis of the problems of communicating the gospel to modern man. It brings together a theoretical (theological) analysis of the problems and a series of concrete examples drawn from newspapers, television, and films.

13. This principle applies equally to the Christian, whether he faces a Moslem or a Marxist. As Joseph Hromadka, the Czech theo-

logian has written, "Theology is, I wish to repeat over and over again, no ideology. It is an effort to interpret, in an adequate and actual way, the Word of the living God and to understand the past, the present, and the future men and history in the light of the divine Word and the divine events. From the perspective of theology as we understand it, all human divisions, systems, social and political institutions, all philosophical thoughts, find themselves on the same level, on the side of the created world in its corruption and promise.

"The dividing line runs not between communists and non-communists. It runs between the Lord of glory and mercy, on the one hand, and human sinners (whether communists or non-communists) on the other. Theologically, it is all wrong to see the main line of division between the Christian ideology and civilization . . . and the non-Christian. . . ." From *Theology Between Yesterday and Tomorrow* by Joseph L. Hromadka, page 67. Used by permission. Unhappily, Hromadka fails to see that this sound theological principle must not prevent one from making real assessments of the various kinds of social institutions on this side of the baseline, capitalist and Marxist alike.

In the same vein, Gerald Cooke has recently written in italics about the encounter with non-Christian religions: *"We must combine witness with exploration within an awareness of vulnerability,"* because no one, including the Christian witness, is invulnerable in the world. *As Christians Face Rival Religions* (New York: Association Press, 1962), page 182.

CHAPTER SIX

*From *The Church's Confession Under Hitler,* by Arthur C. Cochrane. Copyright © 1962, W. L. Jenkins. The Westminster Press, page 262. Used by permission.

**From *Baptist Confessions of Faith,* by W. L. Lumpkin. Valley Forge: The Judson Press, 1959, pages 169-171.

1. The number 666 has endured a steady onslaught of interpretations. Since the writer was addressing his own church, we must look for an appropriate identification from that period. There are many ways of working with this code-name. The method used here relies on the ancient system of counting by using letters instead of ciphers (a=1, b=2, c=3, etc.). When the letters of "Caesar Nero(n)" are counted in Hebrew, they add up to 666.

2. Virtually all the Supreme Court decisions in this area have now been assembled in the useful paperback edited by Joseph Tussman, *The Supreme Court on Church and State* (New York: Oxford University Press, 1962).

3. In an important book, Paul Abrecht discusses the various attitudes of Christians toward the nationalisms of today. *The Churches and Rapid Social Change* (Garden City: Doubleday, 1961), pages 95-112.

4. For this reason, some interpreters prefer to speak of our time as the post-Constantinian era instead of the post-Christian era. This is probably the more accurate way to put it.

5. R. M. Grant, *The Sword and the Cross* (New York: The Macmillan Co., 1955), page 16. This book is a very readable survey of the problem of church and the Roman state until the time of Constantine.

6. The Jehovah's Witnesses fought for the right to refuse to salute the flag and eventually won it from the Supreme Court in 1943 when it reversed its own ruling of 1940.

7. The East German pastor, Johannes Hamel, has seen this clearly: "The fundamental question is this: Does the Christian Church in the Marxist world hear and acknowledge her own gospel in its sovereignty and in all its dimensions? If so, she will receive and accept the Marxist world with its hard realities in the light of the gospel, and she will truly recognize her own situation and undertake her task in this world. Or does the Christian Church understand the powers which rule over her on the basis of a stereotype of ecclesiastical, political, social and cultural traditions? [What we mean by 'Christendom.'] If so, she will neither recognize her own situation nor her own task. Does the Christian Church deny the total sovereignty of the gospel of God over everything in heaven and on earth? If so, she actually grants to the Marxist world to declare and to understand itself as atheistic and to behave accordingly. Or does the Christian Church proclaim publicly and privately . . . that all powers and principalities are already overcome and imprisoned through the resurrection of Jesus Christ? If so, she will reveal the nature of atheism as a forlorn attempt to escape from the reality of the Lord and Creator, or as a kind of forlorn opposition against this reality." Quoted from "The Proclamation of

the Gospel in the Marxist World" in *"How to Serve God in a Marxist Land,* by Karl Barth and Johannes Hamel. (New York: Association Press, 1959), page 84f.

8. The history of missions happily had this side as well as the seamier side of malpractice and misunderstanding. Again and again the gospel has generated movements which produced conflicts. Christendom's missionaries (and their home-base supporters) have been happy to see such conflicts when they are directed against witchcraft or child marriage; unfortunately, they have been less able to see that the same conflicts are inevitable against the white man's rule, however benevolent it may have become. For example, one leaven in African nationalism has been the Bible, for it has brought an understanding of man (every man), a concept of justice (for every man), a conviction that history has a movement, and a meaning (for every man). For a discussion of this, see Abrecht's *The Churches and Rapid Social Change,* page 23ff.

9. What Dawson has in mind is the tendency toward scientific planning, centralized administration, standardization which is part of a technological society regardless of its ideology. Societies complex enough to gear themselves for space navigation are inevitably more and more controlled, that is, more and more in the hands of government. To ask for less government and more rapid progress in space navigation is like asking an elephant to fly. In this sense, all government is becoming totalitarian. Dawson can therefore write ". . . the Nazis and the Communists are not the only totalitarians, they are only parties which have attempted to exploit the totalitarian elements in modern civilization in a simplified and drastic way in order to obtain quick results" (*The Historic Reality of Christian Culture,* page 26).

It is true, of course, that Soviet society is becoming more "open" while ours seems to be under great pressure to be more "closed" to alternatives. If we can keep from mutually annihilating each other, the next-generation farmer, machinist or doctor in the USA and USSR may have much more similar lives than we can foresee now. If so, that will not automatically reduce the conflict of church and state, for that would only mean that the church would live in a state which will be an immense social machine with police power greatly refined by technological advances. In such a situation, Dawson's statement would be perfectly true: "When ultimately a conflict takes place between the new state and the Christian church, it will be far more severe in character than anything that has been known before" (*Ibid.,* page 27).

10. Johannes Hamel puts it with bald correctness: "Whatever may have to be said about Marxism, it is certain that in the encounter with it we do not enter godless territory or a no-man's land outside the reach of the gospel. This is not a province where God's word is neutral, an inferno from which God should save us if he can. On the contrary, as messengers of Jesus Christ we proclaim that through the rise of the Marxist world God has opened for us a new page of his history which began with Easter and ends with the Second Coming." *How To Serve God in a Marxist Land,* page 103. In the same way, Martin Niemoeller, who opposed Hitler's seducing of the church and endured the concentration camp for doing so, has said, "It has taken many years of my life to realize that God is not the enemy of my enemy. . . . He is never the enemy of his enemies." From *The Church's Confession Under Hitler,* page 110.

11. Adapted from Cochrane, *The Church's Confession Under Hitler,* page 222f.

"Thus the whole life of man is one of repentance, not a life of regret but of joyous turning to the forgiver."
p. 76

p 79.
ie God takes us as we are.

The church which ~~practices~~ 'preaches' God's forgiveness must practice its own. p. 80.

p 80. Definition of Forgiveness